FARHANG

BOOK I

FARHANG

BOOK I

Patrick Woodcock

Published by ECW Press
665 Gerrard Street East
Toronto, Ontario, Canada M4M 1Y2
416-694-3348 / info@ecwpress.com

Editor for the Press: Michael Holmes / a misFit Book
Copyeditor: Emily Schultz
Cover design: Jessica Albert
Cover image: "In Leningrad during the siege, people looked like ghosts, and ghosts like people…" 2011, c-print, pastel, pencil, paper, 42.1 x 28.5 cm. © Mihail Chemiakin

LIBRARY AND ARCHIVES CANADA CATALOGUING IN PUBLICATION

Title: Farhang : poems. Book one / Patrick Woodcock.

Names: Woodcock, Patrick, 1968- author.

Identifiers: Canadiana (print) 2023043925X | Canadiana (ebook) 20230439322

ISBN 978-1-77041-751-9 (softcover)
ISBN 978-1-77852-231-4 (PDF)
ISBN978-1-77852-230-7 (ePub)
ISBN 978-1-77852-232-1 (Kindle)

Classification: LCC PS8595.O6397 F371 2023 | DDC C811/.54—dc23

This book is funded in part by the Government of Canada. *Ce livre est financé en partie par le gouvernement du Canada.* We acknowledge the support of the Canada Council for the Arts. *Nous remercions le Conseil des arts du Canada de son soutien.* We acknowledge the funding support of the Ontario Arts Council (OAC), an agency of the Government of Ontario. We also acknowledge the support of the Government of Ontario through the Ontario Book Publishing Tax Credit, and through Ontario Creates.

PRINTED AND BOUND IN CANADA   PRINTING: COACH HOUSE   5   4   3   2   1

In memory of Sherri Decembrini
and for Art and the art to come.

Contents

MONOLITHS

I

What measurements endured? The speed to walk and the speed to run and the hour to liquefy and disappear. There were uncountable fears of woods, of darkness, of language and transport, of the percentage in bottles and the percentage of crime. There was the duration of the beating and the duration of the syllable. There was the distance to the deepest part of the throat, to where *hamzah* and *ha'* were born. The ten articulation points of the tongue and the number of times it should trill. There was the weight of monuments, of ovens and stovepipes, and the data of suffering when coupled in camps. The distance to countries. The distance to cities. The number of stairs sprinted up and down to the train. The arc of the careworn smile on old women selling roses at cemeteries. The depth of the cracks on their buckets and fingers. The number of punctures from thorns. The frequency of the trembling palm peddling cigarettes outside metros midwinter. The width of the base, the height of the stick and the weight of the pyramid atop it in the torture museum.

The moon is 14 237 km away for each year of that time. If he drove to it at 120km/h, there would be off-ramps every 4 ½ minutes to death camps built for only one war. He knows some numbers don't birth libraries, so he works to slow the pace of their extermination, but one can only brake for so long.

II

They engaged like two train wagons, extending their Scharfernberg coupler hands to connect and lock. Their right hands clutched while their left canopied. They spoke passionately so none would think of looking down at them; who looks at non-finito sculptures and praises the unfinished block? Although their bodies appeared calm and ordinary, their fingers connected and disconnected frenetically. They practised for months in the doctor's house after the verdict, but if it did not pass in public it was meaningless. Two fingers and a piece of paper had fallen to the asphalt once. Farhang had panicked and discarded them in the trash, forcing them to sit at the closest café to retrieve the fingers before the bins were emptied; while waiting he felt the damning of his arteries for the first time. They embraced until it was immortalized in the local news as *The Long Goodbye*. They became known in every quarter. Store owners would smirk and yell, *Cherish him!* when they were blocks apart. You could not predict who would visit the jail, so they embraced

below the Fallen Shipyard Workers, the Sun Farer and the Wall of Names, too many walls of names, within soccer pitches that were cemeteries and upon jungle scaffolding to marvel at the clear view of clear felling. They cursed blue skies. Blue skies are yellow, enabling the barbarous in us to see further.

III

He landed in an alphabet with six new letters, and sounds that made him plead for two, plus one, not three. He moved onto the apple tree and the pitch accent when eating boar near the gate of dawn. He found harmony in the whispered and hacked on the metro and read the advertisements on interior car cards aloud. He cleared snow to bellow the epitaphs on poets' tombstones. But to what end? In his head he sang, but his throat only rumbled. He learned that when the word is longer than the line, he must lock the toolshed and walk home. Bless, bless. He imitated the clicked consonants of the Hadza preparing to hunt birds with his father. When one language said it was too hot to work, he played computer hangman to learn the unwritten short vowels; he committed genocide, hanged thousands.

He met Kurds who were fighting to speak their language while trying to define it, who were murdered and tortured for teaching it. Thousands of miles away, Canada's First Nations had their tongues numbed and their birthright's melody muted by a church and state who weaponized their alphabet. For some, language is a hanging snare, a rope with cans, it sounds the alarm before the story drowns, and its voice can no longer glorify. For others, the suffix *vialuk* that means *real, genuine, traditional*, is a soul that refuses to die on a white page without tongue.

IV

He watched water rise and sink back into the ground,
exposing villages and villagers. He saw bridges and
trains jealous of each other, fighting with the push
and pull of time. He saw children running with joy
and from canes. He saw hands that were a
renunciation of flesh. He heard the cough of old men
walking through coal smoke and the sound of the
train that carted them away. He admired the iambic
beat of barking dogs and the molossus march of
hailstorms pounding on corrugated metal. He caught
the quickened gait of the gin-soaked tourist and was
startled by the pop of chicken heads in last year's oil.

To breathe in the air above the treeline is to consume
the purest stimulant. The polar opposite of the desert
bathroom hole or the water closet at memorial sites
in underfunded villages. This is why so many turn to
gluttony to deaden their grief. But what of those
who can't? Who walk all day in want. Is there a
worse touch than that of a child's malnourished
hummingbird hand, one that felt loaned to the limb?
He had brushed the rims of concentration camp
toilets, proved a children's cemetery denied, existed,
but her touch had aged him, calcifying his hate. He
cannot place his senses in abeyance. This is why he
was submerged in the north. He needed darkness and
the right measure of murk. For cloud parting was too
crushing when revisiting and redressing the demons.

V

You sit, stare and rock, slowly, remembering a grandmother's cottage, how warm it felt, and how you airlifted the flotilla of miniature spiders, that you first thought pepper, out of your soup onto the floor. You wouldn't fish them out today, you've learned to wolf down whatever is placed before you. Invigorated, you would offer to go up on the roof to clean the chimney you can't recall existed. But you do remember she first greeted you from atop the roof of her house. Up there in her seventies, haloed by storm clouds, lifted by more of a lattice than ladder.

Around her village were undefended stars, eroding in abandoned cemeteries. Someone needed to cut the grass, raise and level the tombstones. You'd like to return to her, the soup and cemeteries, and stand on the roof where a chimney might have been. You would make one, wider, so she could climb out of it to make the village's children laugh, for you do remember they looked like they needed to laugh. But you can't go back, and she is long dead. You can only hope that someone did believe in both bungalow and *babcia* before they collapsed. You have always had faith in simple stories, like a chimney asking for an old woman to believe in it, and for this woman to ask her visitors to believe in it as well. For without what your memory has fashioned of her, who carried the soup, spiders and ladder? Who warmed this picture?

VI

"Place your hands down." The doctor is awake; the vodka, pills and knife are on the table. Drink and sing, laugh and recite until the pills push in. Sway forward with your forearm extended. Place a ladybug on the table. Quiet. Place your finger on it and push down. Pop. Now to the bone at the base of the finger, pop. Drool onto the floorboard etching, carved after many long nights of sermonizing there. Extend the other. Unclench it. Pop. Now for your drunken brother. Crack. Don't struggle. Pop. Crack. Christ.

You are both back at the table laughing, too drunk and pilled to open the boxes the doctor brought. Ogre steps and maniacal laughter, shoulders up, shoulders down, blood flowing. You will sleep it off after you are bandaged. Tomorrow you will be free to embrace and loathe the informant, judge and jury.

Tonight you must hide. The prosthetics will be here in the morning and you can begin to hug in public again. But for now, bleed and bleat and drink and sing. Soon, you will have a new voice and a printing press in your fingertips. The cell will give you time to regenerate and chronicle what must be labelled an odd life. Riotous? Muddled? But what of those left behind, forsaken to the fog stirred by the fermenting wrecker's ball? There is much left to laud. Here come oceans of wolves, sulphur and coal smoke, then her.

VII

I met him twice a week, on Tuesdays and Fridays. I was never late. We had become the boarded up and defaced corner store locals walked by without a glance. At first, I wore the same tweed suit, tie and shoes, never giving them a reason for a second look. But I had to rethink my approach after a few mishaps and began to wear shirts with absurd double cuffs for more cover. I visited at the same time, and we were allowed to embrace when we greeted each other; his lawyer had demanded this. I'd approach and reach out my right hand to take his. Our left hands and a little of my sleeve would cover them as we exchanged fingers. Our thumbs and ring fingers would pull and disengage the prosthetics, using our palms to help reattach them. My index finger held the miniature pencils and my middle finger held the parchment. His contained the pieces he'd written that week. We made mistakes. Some of the paper stock was too poor to write upon. Some of the pencils broke, forcing him to tap the lead powder out. He would drag the body of the pencil on the cell floor to sharpen then lick before writing. He had received a year for four lines scrawled on a bathroom stall. But a year was a death sentence. We knew a poet's wife who had memorized his work so it would not be burned while he was exiled in correction camps. These poems are all I can summon. His drafts were boxed and cremated, like F—; like we all should be.

VIII (Notes on missing illustrations from text)

They were stippled, shaded and blended beside his writing. Many had trains, some windowless trains. Aerial sketches of concentration camps to capture the scale of systemized hate. A notebook with illegible lines. Holes for toilets, holes for fishing, holes through abandoned airplane tailfins. Holes in the ground to hide mothers and children. Tables for eating, with nothing to eat. Tables for torture, metallic and gleaming. The handle on the bucket that collected the drippings. The choleric and elderly holding expired medication. Decaying teeth, inflamed gums. Tilting beds in tilting houses. Half-dead handshakes by half-dead hands. Eyes, hidden by shade and dusk and cloth. Door handles to houses of worship collapsing. Concrete scars from mortar shells. The myriad of eyes behind tenement walls. Racist graffiti with racist grammar. The garden hose clung to when descending into mines. The glare of the wandering and the grin on the men who made them wander. Unscalable fences and those pinned by their sword tips. Fishing vessels and shipyards. The dour faces of those who sold cigarettes for the baby beside them. Archaeological dig sites, dusted ribs, partial skulls. The permanent shadow burned into concrete after self-immolation. The tip of the cross poking out of snow-covered graveyards. He drew them so they'd begin to rot and fade. This was his salvation; he had to watch what should die, dying.

PHARMAKOI

AND

FILAMENTS

1. The birth and suicide of my Peter Shaw

Was the purling panorama of the post-Victorian
womb undone? Did his birth by blunder stun?
        Why did he
chew and champ through the nuchal chord,
its running knot and running joke?
        Why did he
toss it like a collegiate scarf around his throat?
        Why did he
crawl in and out of train windows, quicker
than the stench and stretch of those watching
or the watchmen pissed and parading
        through coal smoke at dawn?

II

He rode the harlequinade like a horse, trotted
and trundled like a muddled marionette.
He was born of the wheeled and wheeling,
the crabbing and cocked, until he left
the pulsing panorama of the pediatric tomb
to rock within the chug chug chug of train
and pint, for another's song, another's story,
another's moonlight when waterfalling to sleep.

        The applausive clicks cascading the air
        were passengers bolting their doors,
        as your unquiet quietly stared
        at your shadow now sweeping the floor.

2. I leaned my head upon the window to watch clouds

as gashed as old kitchen pots, loitering in the sky
like what was once pushed out the crematoriums
                we neared.
When our driver stopped to piss we watched
another, standing and cursing, flailing in a rage
at the deceptiveness of clouds and the virga
taunting his land. When the first drops struck
                we thrust our heads out to be cleansed
and watched him fade into the fathoms he detested.
I courted clouds all day and surveilled the motes
transported upon rails of sunlight in each room.
Cloudspotting was my reprieve from what lay
within the borders of a new Canada. I peered
out windows to avoid searching for paired shoes
and felt ill when I saw the clouds part so a worm
moon could approach our taxi stand like the light
                on another train with more footwear.

Three decades later, the clouds that mothered me
                act as a firewall between children
and the toys flown by foreigners. Armies no longer
need clouds to harbour their contempt. We bomb
and burn from blue skies now, creating puffs
from the picnicking whose ashes are then collected
to drift within an ossuary that will transport them
back onto the fields of men who want to forget
how some clouds come to be and the weight within,
                above and below them.

3. Enough snow had fallen to prove he was alone

There was no groundskeeper, no guard. No one.
The wrought iron gate implanted in the entryway
stood like a sundial, its top hinge hanging and tolling
for none. It was the second relic he'd navigate
and far sturdier than the drunkard still cursing
from the bus stop. It was the stillness that made him
uneasy. He nervously tried to conduct the clutter
and chirp of birds, to unstill their whistling and wings
while summoning squalls to rattle the woods
encircling him. By mid-afternoon he felt the weight
of the lowering sky; it looked like a coffin's cap panel,
full of the malicious softness a camp guard's smile
and helping hand possessed.

While finger framing the kitchen and the SS Clubhouse,
he tripped backwards and shook his head in disgust
when he recrossed his footprints and saw their lack
of depression. He crawled the operating room's floor
and closed one eye below the stainless-steel tables
to imagine the drip — measured the distance between
the rabbit hutches and crematorium. At the hollowed
monument, he removed his jacket and shirt to place
upon the glass. He felt hundreds of eyes waiting to see
whose jawbone would be snapped — he chose the ghost-
white little one. In reality, no one watched or cared
if this moment was caught in natural light. His time
would soon be dusted away as the camp returned to its
underexposed haze.

4. Michael's dive

Did you leap or back-roll like a scuba diver,
with as little energy left for life as its rebuttal?
Did your ankle strike a ledge and each cloud become
an entangled chute spiralling with you in free fall?
        Panicked, did you tear at your clothes,
or did you stand straight, raise your arms and push off
the platform, tight and precise? What was your angle
        of entry when you ripped into the concrete?

No one spoke to me at your funeral. Kept
at a distance, I decided to take you for one last flight.
        We joined swifts and starlings to circle
the puppet theatre, opera house and Świdnicka Cellar;
it was a greater trinity to honour than the one offered
        by the bearded ruin singing of your sin.

I think of you often since I have known too many
idolaters of the dive. But lately you have wrested away
from my invitations. There is no longer any wonder
or joy in your eyes when we hover above the priests
and parishioners we mocked as young men. I am now
forced to drop my trousers to soil the frenzied zeal
of tourists in the old town, alone, while you curse
        the wreckage of your car and the blood
on the headrest that dries and dampens over and over.

Before it is my turn, tell me, did you find the tonic
for what you fled? Was the pavement dear, tender?

5. A Wieliczka horse in motion (The circularity)

He only wants to be wind-beaten again, and not circling
within their time — to gallop out of this gloom,
glossy and untethered —
freed from the subterranean travesty
where the weight of political plots
amongst pillars of salt
rests upon royalty
winding into
windless time, raising
and lowering the morally arched and physically
frail.

Longing for moon blindness, he felt
ashamed when his spine
began to sink
like the pulverized eggshell in an hourglass.
His pendulous testicles, the harbingers
of death, ticked and tormented him
as he struggled with the volt:
Arbeit Macht Frei
for he hadn't seen: *zun, słońce, Sonne, солнце*
in years.

They should have demined the gnomon, let him gallop
before being hacked for stew. Fleshed or not, his bones
and shadow deserved far more cabinet cards
than Occident,
or any other horse in motion.

6. Finally, the truth

At midnight, two half-manned monstrosities
fled a fog of cloying thickness by pounding
on a red door until the drunken bosun let them
climb up and onto hardwood floors as slippery
           and slipshod as a warship's deck —
covered in such an abundance of spittle, bile
           and brine they had to slide as if skating.
They sat until daybreak, trying to persuade him
they were artists, a notion he refused. Drunk
and depleted, the oldest acquiesced and said
           they imported Polish dolls to Canada.
The owner slowly raised his head and smiled:
                    Finally, the truth.

For the next five months, no one talked to them
about the ladies and gentlemen of Borowski,
the breakfast poems of Lipska or the scrawled
           list of stimulants on Witkiewicz portraits,
but they were introduced to derelict dollmakers
and shown sketches of limbs and prototypes.
They feigned interest with nods as they listened
to the polemical debate of porcelain over plastic
           and left when the contrarians
collided with the sodden floor, creating ripples
in the slopline with their curses and questions:
Tell me the truth. How could they not know about
           the rose petal horizon
                    on a Kashubian skirt?

7. We watched him dance

He opened the front door and street-level bay window
to create a wind tunnel to awaken his untucked shirt.
      After clearing the room and hardwood floors
a record was placed on the turntable; he closed his eyes
      and sighed with the sleeve he shelved. He rushed
back to the window to close the curtains — commuters
were arriving for the next bus. The rings' metallic shriek
and matador tear of the cloth panicked the pigeons
      atop the shelter into a fecal flood narrative.

      He began climbing the Tatras,
stumbling with outstretched arms, catching entire snowfalls
      lowered upon his land by others.
He descended and bent over to plant trees, one at a time,
      until 1914 demanded a forest.

He changed clothes while whirling within the particles
and exhaust fumes sweeping in from the street, imported
hats, epilates and medals, farmed near Słupsk, then swam
      out into the Baltic to heave in an old submarine
to dance for the soldiers bloated and buried within it.
He turned lovingly while miming the century's fatigue,
a history of invasions. By dawn, the amphetamine
      and amphitheatre had weakened — we wrestled
our nightmares into song and slur, attacking the tank
of our terrors on horseback; shouting until the vastness
of the new day died. Then, after a new line or two,
      he began to ascend with Blue Note again.

8. The dangling light bulb and the constellations created

You hid your leg under the table and sat
with your back to the wall
after a long morning of writing — asking others
to fetch your drinks
so they would not see you limp.
You rested, pant leg rolled up —
never high enough.
Sometimes you feigned boredom,
pinching the denim of your jeans
between your thumb and forefinger
to pump small pockets of air around the burns
on your calf. Later that evening,
after a few more sips at home,
you admired the colours and domes
in your bedroom mirror. So many plays
could be written about the curve of the cicatrix.
You admired how a sunrise on your thigh
blended into a sunset on your ankle
and how the scattered islands of blisters
looked like the Shield of Sobieski.

The electric typewriter was a gift from an engineer
who had placed a light bulb and socket
in the middle of the cord to drop its current.
Beneath the desk it swayed and bounced
when you daydreamed and rocked, branding you
back to a world where your poems never glowed
as bright as the bulb or burn.

9. Where in god's name is Frank Zappa's bloody 17-foot head

An hour,
no, four,
through parks
and lanes
as snow
swam down
my neck
and back
with maps
torn through,
by winter
winds. *Bell's*
palsy is
the face
of this.
My clapper
tongue
by noon
was done,
my limbs,
too numb,
succumbed
to loss,
but when I saw
you're half
a cross,
enraged,
I tried a caber toss.

10. He placed his mother on the balcony in winter for a few litas

(The world's largest goldfish, *Carassius auratus*,
was discovered on a tenement balcony in Vilnius,
Lithuania, in 1995. "Motina," as it was called,
was evicted so her son could rent her tank
to a more affluent and ornamental clownfish.)

Still awake at 5am, the wreckage sat and stared
at the imperfect winter morning, pressing his nose
on the window to thaw a fisheye through the ice.

He watched the snow begin to shuffle, rise and roam
from roof to balcony and back, squinting to admire it
darting and dancing, turning in upon itself before
                bursting skyward like a white stork.

At first it was a few locks of alabaster hair that fell
from under the orange tarp on the balcony, flapping
in the wind like a torn dorsal spine, as if the candles
not the flames had decided to let their essence arc
                and flit. He was forced to search
for a lighter to fight back against the wind and snow
                recrystallizing his porthole. As the opening
enlarged, five smoke-stained fingers, like elongated fry,
                emerged to hold down the tarp.

Other winds from other lanes arrived to constrain her
before rattling him and the window frame: *Let her go*.
                He let her go.

11. No one touches frames anymore

We all withdrew to the simpler shadows, to wait
        for her liver to lurch toward sardines
and spirits; then we pressed against you, caressed

and undressed your waves with our fingertips,
feigning auscultation to thrust into the ogees
encircling *Ships in a Storm, Bracing the Waves*
        and *Hurricane at the Sea.*

We plunged ourselves into the frame's flesh,
        exploring its flutes and scrolls
with filleted fingers, deboned to thrust further
into the semi-circles of its circus-yard Cyrillic.

We pilfered and plundered one stiletto nail
at a time, carting away the shavings within
        hand-painted porcelain thimbles.

*

        No one touches frames anymore.
The Tretyakov stretches the ocean floor, carried
within submarine cables; and the old gallery guards
in their new naval dress are shrunken and seated
on Russian remora, guiding and nudging the sharks
from their target, from carving and cutting the wood
we've forgotten, from tearing our frames with each
        shake of their head.

12. Lenin

It was a non-day, a false day, a pale winter's day
when two-thirds of one's time felt forged,
the store windows and idling cabs, unapproachable.
The walk involved ducking around tilted scaffolding,
unkempt babushkas and toothless monoliths.
He had to run away from the icebreakers pushing through
intersections where ambulances had to await green.
He hid in a park until he had consumed enough courage
to turn on the shadows that had turned on him.
Whatever this moment was, it was not his.
The city's Russian grew monstrous,
each word was monumental, an elongated wink,
a Peter the Great travesty.
The management of time was kept by an hourglass
bladder that turned every ten minutes.
There were no bathrooms, just empty alleyways to clear
and restart the clock. After a few more blocks into the depths
of the day were stumbled, a piranha was purchased,
placed in its carrying tank and baptized
Lenin.
He floundered back to MGU like a ruined salesman,
terrifying everyone who came within spitting distance
of the convulsing suitcase that would be frozen solid
within an hour. That evening a vigil was held in his room.
Lenin rested peacefully on the window ledge, surrounded
by candles and mourners while Vysotsky sang
into the courtyard: *That's it, I've decided,*
I'll drink some tea and die . . .

13. Holy water from Trinity Lavra smells rancid

Saint Sergius, what a smell.
I cannot see. I cannot sleep.
The surge, the swell, the nostril's tell.
The nonmonastic bottled swill.
The godforsaken grinding shrill
of runners, monks and all who plod:
           "Drink as if approaching God!"

Lord, Sergius, what a smell.
I cannot sleep. I cannot breathe.
The terror, the roar, the hellfire psalm.
The arboraceous atom bomb.
The matryoshka's martyrdom. "These woods
are false; the dolls who greet us, are no more
           than a coffin's fetus."

Bartholomew, what a smell.
I cannot breathe. We cannot see.
The douters dimmed the candle's quest
to darken icons. Are your blessed
mere forgeries who cross their chest?
"Their legs and souls will soon grow numb;
           below their coats, just rot and worm."

If Mongol hordes are in the font,
the sacrarium their pit latrine, hold the doll
at seven cast, discard the child
           to nest me last.

14. A dead woman and a dead poet in Vagankovo Cemetery

Old women in wheelchairs should not be abandoned
beneath umbrellas, or hidden
behind tilting tombstones.
        I circled the mausoleum sheltering you
        and thought: old women in wheelchairs
        hidden by umbrellas

must be rescued from Russian cemeteries.
I cleaned the serpentine tops
of your neighbours, and scanned
        the graveyard while my fingers
        turned within the Cyrillic etchings
        of epitaphs and names.

I inched through the snow and narrow pathways
like a suicidal before their legs
were ledgeless, to prove you were,
        and were not. I indexed your broken
        left tire, the left caster that was missing,
        how your ankle tilted

from the footrest and how your sock concertinaed,
leaving a few inches of skin
coquettishly unveiled.
        You were as white as the snow I brushed
        from the bust of another. I gave you his
        flowers, then recited a few lines about
        a shabby overcoat before walking home.

15. I joined John at 12:24 to walk with Dostoevsky

I purchased roses three times before finding
what should have been grander, for I'd seen
tank-sized tombstones in Moscow's graveyards.
To prove the scale of your skull was slander,
I opened your gate and switched heads with you.
Only one fieldfare answered the birdsong
of its hinges. I walked out, bearded and bent
on mocking the city that supported this.

I met a friend, who showed no interest in how I
altered my stride and posture to support your head,
or how whatever I drank ran down my chin.
Although my walk was cumbrous, my arms flailed
like thuribles tied to a windmill's sails. I offered
three double swings over children hiding
from kennels in alleys as pedo-priests offered
tickets to the compline's after party.

With a newly adopted anti-amble and pages torn
from an old guidebook, we sought out
the apartment where one thought to still Rasputin.
The first door opened to a dollmaker's morgue,
where we bribed our way to another's. By dusk
the weight of our quest and my skull had taken
its toll. When I fell through his gate mumbling
something about dying and corn and fruit, his lips
parted and pleaded for one final walk before our
reheading at Semyonovsky Square.

I purchased my first watch at 11pm

Lenin's face rested behind hands dead
within hours. To repair him I boarded a train
to the Black Sea and offered it to the Sturgeon
Horological Society. After resurfacing at dawn, his
sarcophagus was smashed by a taxi's side mirror and
tossed. My first Matryoshka was Russian writers. At dusk
I sat with the infirm near the Neva and drank vodka from
Dostoevsky's head until an enraged drunkard cracked Tolstoy
off of my leg for not refilling him to the nasal tip. I returned
to the Black Sea, weighted it with pebbles and covered it in
Mariinsky posters and stickers. I delivered it to the Sturgeon
Malyutin Memorial Society. The lesser writers rested within
my coat pockets. While exploring estuaries I thumb flipped
Goncharov like a poker chip and knuckle rolled Bulgakov
to amuse children. I found Leo bobbing at dawn. I bought
my first edition of poetry in the metro at 9am, a miniature
edition of Mayakovsky. But when freed from their cases,
the pages flew around the city like a trembling of siskins
that took me hours to capture before the last night train.
The following day I boiled sounds and dipped pages
in isinglass. The last lines I recall binding were:
But it seems, before they can launch a song,
poets must tramp for days with callused
feet . . . the sluggish fish of the imagination
*founders softly in the slush of the heart.**
Or something like that. Christ knows. It was years ago.
In my dreams I still drink from skulls with fishmongers
and book conservators, but we all look so old, so tired.

17. The lowering

Above the city and the ocean
were moon-caught moments, glaciered
and signalling about a way for me to grapple
with the fall, before I knew what the fall was
and who it would pummel.
It was not my devotional decay,
but a general weakening
as my world sensed
her lowering.
Our guide tried to circumnavigate
the grim gradient of crevices that surrounded us
by studying his computer,
as a doctor would x-rays. A misread spot,
or hidden line could be fatal.
He deflated the tires
so we could climb higher. I stood outside,
trying to breathe in everything that sparkled
as he reattached one that had fled the rim
with aerosol and flame. After we reached the summit,
we were told that our Jeep was being tracked
and had a large hook on the back
so we could be pulled out of a crevasse
by a helicopter if we plunged in.

But there were no hooks on her, chemo only
slowed the slide. After the computer screen darkened
and there was no glimmer of her goodness upon it,
no helicopters came.

18. On the first day Kristján welcomed me, molten rock

and lava performed as Hekla trolled the landscape.
He showed me how a bowed guitar could sound
like a thousand trombonists at war in the song cave.
He summoned blue and yellow ladders to rise
from the streets so I could see the haven beside
Selfljót river and the *Lava at Bessastadir*. I heard
the euphonies of sagas used to fight The Great Edict
and learned not all poets spend their lives falling.
          He inspired me to dream

of a squadron of helicopters lowering symphonies
into extinct volcanoes, to compose Skaldic verse
to the clicking of studded tires tearing our street
apart mid-spring, to open my windows and inhale
the warm notes from the cello being played
in the cemetery, and then wave to the revivified
corpses and sculptures walking to the ocean
          to intertwine with the kelp.

But there was an ugliness we didn't see — seeds
were being planted where they shouldn't be — in towers
trombones and skulls, tearing down our ladders,
grounding helicopters, dead weighting our wonder.
I was wrong to mourn you. You awakened the magma
under E15, sending meltwater to move the grieving.
When we all collide in 10 000 years, our atoms will
reassemble in craters to sing of our slipping back
          from the quiet.

19. Dreaming on Jón Páll Sigmarsson's Tombstone

On those rarest of days when the wind and ice
bears grew mischievous, he poured concrete
into whatever walked to heave into the ocean
          and create waves for romantics.

He travelled to Spain to pull swords from bulls;
placed them in the matador's mouth so he
could be swung until the foolishness of his faith
          fell out.

Fishing boats were hauled in and balanced atop
a muleta's stick and spun for the children sitting
without power.
                    He consumed glaciers to lower
his body temperature and drank reservoirs
so those trapped within floodplains could learn
          of Tree-foot's battles.

He bellowed Laxness at Þingvellir to rattle halls
and built a great bridge of whale skulls to reach
the barrel moon. He would churn it until the sagas
          it had stolen poured out.

He taught us to bury our faces beside puddles
and clumps of grass to see the oceans and forests
within our reach. But he was only this mountain
briefly. After his muscles raised rivers, his body
          blued as something deep within ruptured.

20. I did not ask to enter your house

or hop the fence that looked like film
violently torn from the canister. I didn't
climb onto your roof to rejoice within
the lonely choriamb of its chimneys
                and muntins.
I did not ask for the curtains to be cut
and candles to be lit. I wanted nothing
done to the colours I saw upon arrival;
the whites that colonized your acreage
or the browns and greys of the semi-trees
and patches of rock trailing upward into
the twist and twirl of frozen fog, to be
                flushed or retouched.

        Halldor of this winterhouse,
I didn't knock. But I did count five
gatherings of windows with four crosses
and cursed the surge of emptiness I felt
        when seeing you as one.

I was not sure it was yours. I barely knew
my driver. I had hoped for goats and farms
torn from Louisa's landscape. For you
to open your door to say: *Come to the fire
in my miserable dwelling*. But it was still
a grand day, bitter cold, filled with fog
and the purest grey. If only you'd seen
        how excited I was . . .

21. Sometimes trampolines are made of cello

        medleys and cemetery moss.
Sometimes trampolines are made of twigs
        and grass and insects
within caves where Kurds have to arc
        their necks when aloft.

Sometimes trampolines are made of bellies,
        blanched and bloated,
floating down rivers or walking to schools.
        Sometimes trampolines
are made of lettuce leaves and garbage bags,
        in clogged drainage ditches.

Sometimes trampolines are made of tires
        and corrugated metal, blown
off of overflowing cinderblock homes.
        Sometimes trampolines
are only the remains of trampolines, discarded
        by the pearly and gated.

Sometimes trampolines are made of the bones
        and concord of old birds
who inspired rainclouds withholding rain
        to elasticize the land.
But most modern trampolines are made from
        the stretched fabric of time,
for men with light skin, who want to deliver
        their uproar from above.

22. Two men slouched through Sarajevo at midnight

in a midwinter glow, trying to free themselves
from what made the evening unpleasant; groping
for a path through streets where bestial shadows
rubbed against garbage bins.
It grew darker; their vision limited. It was a battle
against the moaning silhouettes and snowflakes
misleading them. One of them reassembled
the dented trombone he'd purchased from a bar
to simulate the sound of a civil defence siren.
They hoped someone would battle through
the echoes to aid them. No one came.
They found an alley whose dead-end curved
into an acoustic shell that elongated the stumbling
slide's embouchure beautifully.
The police, who arrived after the last guttural pulse
pushed its way through the oceanic old town,
only wanted the world of warbles and whistles
disassembled. They cared little about Sarajevo
growing subaquatic. After the bell tube and slide
were shoved back into their coats, they climbed
to a small bar in the euphotic zone to reassemble
their alarm. The last legato lament sent ripples
throughout the city. When the cops returned, none
were left to wave. They'd emptied their water keys
and gone to sit with a couple who muttered about
a time when they were flooded by repulsive radio
waves. A time when the world's police left them
to drown in watering holes of fear and doubt.

23. Lemon's vaudeville

It was mid-spring when I first appreciated
you in boxer shorts, debating your shadow
and its reflection in the bank window.
Like fantoccini freed from their wires
and quickened by amphetamine, you sought
a greater audience. Post-grad milquetoast
smoked and adjusted their caps before
unclothed boutique mannequins while you
coerced a scourge of mosquitoes to reshape
       into the first helicopter battalion.
When the applause faded you mechanized
the clouds and semaphored them into
       Stari Grad.

       You placed a lemon in your mouth
and grabbed an old shopping cart to shuffle
off toward the old city where you hoped
both citrus and cirrus would halt the sharp-
shooters — roaming the streets until a tinge
of yellow appeared in both sniper and sky,
forcing some to adjust their telescopic
       and patriotic views.
Along with the united front caster's keening
that echoed throughout the valley, your yellow
moon rind soaked in saliva bewildered them;
so it was left, like you, to rot on its own.
A sign with *Taxi* written in pen flapped
       like a loose Band-Aid on your cart.

24. No one cares if rats explode

The barbed wire encircling the school
was as absurd as the headmaster's clothing.
Both were good ol' boy Americana, a flotilla
of edges and points to fence in the school
grounds or neck. My children were sitting
in the garden of Mr. McGregor when I heard
it burst. You never forget the tenor and tin
of your first pop and yelp while attempting
to mute the landmine's elation with audio
             books about rabbits.

When Samuel Whiskers arrived, trained
to scuttle and scamper through the fields
in a squalid spring offensive, children
no longer cried. Who cares if a rat dies?
He returned every evening to umbrella
their universe in anti-handling explosives,
fluffing and tossing the fields and valleys
like blankets, concealing mine upon mine.

No dogs would return to end these horrors.
The children lay still as he crawled upon
their beds to place bounding mines beneath
their pillows and blankets as his tripwire tail
tickled their noses. Why was a dog's whimper
unbearable? He donned his green coat, yellow
vest and left them to the demise of their dog
             days and dog-delighted lives.

25. Our lady of the unlit, half-lit whole

Before falling and kneeling like you,
I toured your countryside's vineyards
to collect and consider what I needed
to insult the softness of your sacred soil.

I walked across Medjugorje to St. James
where I whistled and clapped to assess
its acoustics. I circled you in an infidel's
carriage while auditioning to welcome
the next apparition. I was borne again,
tripped up by hollows and furrows, until
a pit in an unlit alley took me; altar wine
is blood from the falling in, crawling out.

Earlier, on the hills, where the flushed
awaited the redeemer, I was a heaven-
reacher, bowing sarcastically. By dusk
I was raging for rubbing alcohol to be
driven down into my exposed ankle bone.

Far from Mary, far from a hospital, far
from immaculate, I waited for spirits
to redress the wrongs of the day. I gazed
out of the car to the mountains for a sign
but only saw the gormless grin of a half-
man, half-weeping icon, the falsity of his
tears was attacked with religious fervour
               by the wind and rain striking back.

26. Mourning by association

The falsity of funerals was learned at St. Jude's.
Between hymns I spotted them, those not made
for mourning. They stirred like they were sitting
in armour, longing for rain to lust after the organ
so they could whisper to their mistresses. Some
would draw attention to the stained glass Christ
        while tapping their watch impatiently.

A child of six saw through this. The affectation
of their cane's faux-ivory ferrules. The knees
never touching the kneeler, for an embroidered
handkerchief from their country club was placed
upon it. I saw a ghastliness next to cleanliness.

From the roof of the Holiday Inn, Darko and I
watched thousands of umbrellas converge around
the old parliament building and admired how they
blended into an oscillating oil slick of an ocean.

Occasionally the wind would shuttle a few toward
the old town, to be returned by the animated punts
of a pre-teen collective. A sad, ragged yellow one,
overturned and weighted by rainwater, limped below
the mourners, reflecting them in its putrid pool. In it,
the impatient ones were seen brooding and desperate
to stay spotless. Below their loathing, lipstick stained
        cigarette butts, like little planes, sailed
within clouds that passed judgment by moving on.

27. How wrong we were — a private bar in Sarajevo

As Tito, Tom and Jerry opened their doors,
we locked ours. Carting notebooks and pens
I would descend the mortarless cobbled lanes
of Trebević, past the echoes of goats and rank
       religious noises
as scoundrels on illegal scaffolding trickled
down to bloody the village vagrant, discarding
him at his sister's gate where he would be
uncoiling like a snail's neck when I passed.
He would be stomped again before dawn.

Dusk was a good time to enter empty parks,
to swing and swig and wait for the final text
calling me down. It was an aesthetic crusade,
this march made by ten or more, twice daily,
three times on Fridays. We owned disposable
egos and the bridges burnt were of no concern
       to the Miljacka
or long march home. What our piss penned
       was flushed and binned.

Busts of Tito, Tom and Jerry tablecloths and
curtains are what I remember. Not one story.
Admiral's voice has been buried. How wrong
we were. Passion and poetry never outlive
plastic adornments and dime store figurines.
We should have carved verse into our teeth,
       our rapture into our fillings.

28. Portions of food are subject to the cook's hatred of George W

On his first day they left an uncooked
grain of rice. No cutlery. No napkins.
He carried it into his room and sailed
it upon the ocean of his tea, stirring it
until dawn prayer stopped his journey.
He drank the ocean, the ship and cargo
        it carried.

The next morning, he awoke, hungry,
and left to walk the wadi to the souk,
hoping to annul his cravings by self-
immolation. He returned to the distant
and untalkative who scorned his *Salam*.

Another uncooked grain of rice was left
and launched into his tea and stirred,
so savagely the ship and a wave or two
spilled onto the rug. Disgusted, he left
        them dry like the riverbed.

On his third day he rolled the television
below the air conditioner, no longer
caring for rice and tea, daydreams or dry
riverbeds. Spent, he still had the capacity
to curse and condemn the 41st charlatan
in a long line of charlatans. He cried out
and blasphemed, oblivious to the men
and stockpiles of food arriving at his door.

29. Shade

There was no shade but under one tree,
and I intended to harvest squares of it.
They would be sold in the souk beside
tea and spices and slipped into one's

wallet for bus rides when the windows
were nailed shut and the air conditioner
broken. I would create misbahas to carry
and finger when the heat was stifling.

There would be exclusive cuts for men,
women and the Bangladeshi workers
thirteen to a room. The stones caressed
by this umbra were for the less affluent.

I would have it hammered and thinned
into head scarves and swaddling blankets.
I would walk to the souk to sell smaller
squares to enwrap sugar cubes and cakes.

But for the unfaithful,
it will be driven into the darkness of their
lust, deep between the legs of the woman
they hide; with whom they explore an ache
withheld from the one who lives without
shade, deep within hell; who'll be blamed
and banished for the sickness planted
by her husband's adultery and frigid seed.

30. Black spectres darted across the asphalt artery

like hooked fish jerked out of the water, pectoral fin
dishdashas flapping in the wind. It was impossible
to manage these desert tributaries. We almost hit two
dozen of the black-robed carp who disappeared back
into the caliginous coastline. Forced to wait and turn
off our engines, we watched currents of sand frolic
and flicker within our headlights, animated by those
sprinting and others collecting the assas and muzzars
             shed during the sprint.
He appeared under the smirk of the jaundiced moon,
standing in the middle of the road, in a white gown
reradiating our high beams, inflating like a floating
bell until he was a supermoon. He beckoned with arms
that ebbed and flowed until he was the jellyfish, moon
and tides. He held us, but refused to acknowledge
the Minister of Fisheries Wealth, or the Department
of Astronomical Affairs. He showed no interest in the
scholars and artists documenting him so they could
dissect and diminish him for the sultanate by morning.
After a wave to Capricorn, he tore down the moon
and heaved it like a boomerang so we'd turn and duck
while he deflated and darted out of our depth of field.
             It is lonely, living the life of a highway martyr,
chasing your faith as it fades like a tail light in the desert,
or fish's tail into the depths. The man who stopped us
wanted to give those running from darkness to darkness
a little less to fear. Shouldn't they be allowed to explore
             the depths without being lit and hit by skeptics?

31. Hemoptysis kiss

I

Petrochemical sunsets storm the mouth
and swell the tongue as if scorpion-stung.
Raw and torn and sandstorm scraped, your
bloodied gums and bloodied palm string
the dusk and stretch the dawn then thrum
and drum and pump the land, pump the lung,
        pump the hand.

II

Hours will be spent, washbasin bent, purging
and cursing the flaring and carnal, as twilight
        and methane vie for the vestal.
While those who set fires, with muddled desires
for the curve of the flame and sunset's pelisse,
        gasp as they grip, thrust and release.

III

A tailfin with two swords will slit the sky's
throat. You must slaughter the sky as you'd
slaughter a goat. Fly into flames as stones fly
below. Saudia must burn. Saudia must glow.
Bloodlust, money, feud and line must plummet
and perish,
               no more intertwine.

32. They were in the shadows, waiting in cells

when I walked through manmade woodlands,
          dressed in black, like a cheap
Northrop knockoff. But stealth bombers don't
have plastic wheels that chime like metal bars
on toy xylophones or get gravel and melting
gum jammed in them. After thirty minutes
          I had to drag it like a stubborn child.
I purchased water, oranges and potatoes, a Brit,
the yeast and bins and a Frenchman, the sugar
and broom handles. The weight of my cargo
on the scorching concrete melted the wheels
          off my suitcase in an hour.
I had to carry the child, now sleeping, home.

Around the same time I was pushing through
          the woods to my compound,
my father was carrying my mother back down
a trail to his truck in Algonquin Park. Her bones
were done. Cancer, like Al Qaeda, had waited
long enough; her sleeper cells had all activated.
I went to bed, oblivious to the sickness in some
that would soon surround me. Years later, I saw
a man carrying kindling and felt ill when he left
a piece that fell. To be of use was all it wanted,
to help light and warm a room. We are judged
by what we carry and discard. It is a lie that we
don't bring it with us. We do. Its weight helps
          most of the world descend.

33. Machete fights at sunrise are lovely

Machete fights sounded like a mother
kissing her baby, the little peck upon
the cheek or heavier one on the brow.
Even the cats and toads, pariah pups
and birds were enthralled as I was

when cars arrived to deliver matriarchs,
who were paid in rank meat, to sweep
the acres of broken glass. But they had
to wait for the last slap of the open blade

to land and the alleys and storefronts
to grow gracious again. The sun's rays
turned the tienda's table into a shield
from the crusades, a radiating cross
of stainless steel reflected the clouds.

Momentarily orphaned children tried
to recreate the fight's tone by lobbing
pebbles onto the corrugated metal roof
of a kiosk. But theirs was a gentler kiss,
like the one a mother would lower upon
            the coffin of her child.

We slowly withdrew when the rain
and police arrived to cleanse the street
of all that sparkled. The blades sat on
the floor. None died, or were done for.

34. The smile

I walked through the arrival doors in Medellín
with a backpack covered in foam and dry powder.
Our plane had caught fire on the runway in Ibagué.

I have always been a poor passenger, not outwardly,
but within the heart, head and bladder. I had feared
for my health while our plane's cargo hold burned
and raised toasts to each fire engine that appeared,
limply applauding for those tearing our bags out.

We departed after our luggage, clothes and plane
were covered in fire foam. While I was spreading
toothpaste under my nose to soften the stench,
a fellow passenger asked why we hadn't changed
planes; the flight attendant smiled and quickened
her pace; she hid until we were descending. Over
thirty-five years before, on a preschool bus, a boy
unfastened a fire extinguisher and coated my face.
The thought of this simple act of rebellion raised
            my Crest chevron.

We flew so low I could see children in uniforms
gathering for their bus. I wanted our plane to end
above them and grinned at the thought of my jelled
moustache smashing through their windshield.
It might not be funny at first, but in a few decades,
who knows? We all need something to smile about
when the plane of our life is on fire or plummeting.

35. Why shouldn't the gunwale be an inch

above the water? It made it easier to dip
my hands to wash the monkey urine off
my neck and jacket. While I pretended
to row, my fingertips, like topwater lures,
bobbed on and out, above the piranhas.
I loved the thrill of squinting and melding
the jungle and shoreline. I used my paddle
to reshape reflections, insert jet streams
and trigger turbulence. A twist of my oar
sent whirlpools of algae into the ether.

        Three days earlier, a missionary
boat had drifted past us. We saw no one,
heard no voices, no engine; not a sound
came from the two-story chapel drifting
the Amazon with a crooked rood and roof.
But we knew they were hiding and waiting
to make a bloody mess of it all. Hidden
behind Nordic Cross curtains, they lusted
        after the innocent and malleable.

        Piranhas can be forgiven for their
uneucharistic sharing of flesh, but clergy
should be caught and placed in the gossip's
bridles they used to silence. Let them hold
        their tongues as their church sinks;
as a shoal of parishioners rush to them
        for a Biblical feeding frenzy.

36. After unsnagging her belt from the mosquito net

she descended her middle bunk's ladder
and ran into the Amazon's modest morning,
dream-drained and fleeing the taxing lectures
            from pretentious Mennonites.
She had no apologies left; each stumble was
blamed on the forest floor. It was a time to lift
and lower, nothing more. When we saw the red
phallic roots on a tree trunk being finished off
by a symphony of caterpillars, we all cringed,
            and she made her first wail of the day.

By hour two we had run out of water and began
to trip as scopophobia slipped into our group.
Tree roots pulsed. We swore blood pumped
through them. Centipedes created living chalk
outlines of a murder we believed happened
moments before our arrival. We were covered
in cuts and bleeding when we emerged. Only
one of us was smiling, admiring how her filthy
arms hung like the vegetation we failed to still.

The village elder, who'd travelled to London
to lecture on Indigenous medicine, only offered
warm beer, no water, and contorted his arms
into boto chasing catfish. I jerked backwards
when offered his hand for his arm swung at me
like a downed power line; we smiled until
            our laughter matched the jungle's.

37. Dehydrated hallucinations and the houses they build

The tree trunks looked like a distended baby's belly,
their roots, like octopus tentacles, stretched across
the jungle's floor. There were thousands, like barbed
wire, around the manor house I willed from the land.

A wall of mosquitoes formed a syringe to puncture
the birthday balloon, weighted by a monkey's head,
lumbering across the lawn. A man yelled for a child
to stop rubbing her face: it angers them, he warned.
        But it was too late, they dug, she bled.

I was tapped on the shoulder and told to drink more
water. I had none. Our guide smiled when I asked
how much longer the manor house would match my
        pace. I pushed on.

More children arrived, twelve, one in each window,
waving to me with candle flame bodies. When I tried
to outrun them, I turned into a branch and cut open
        my cheek and ear. I bled. I begged to be left

so I could attend to whatever I believed was wrong.
When the father saw my pain, he offered a ladder out
of my entanglements. *Go up there, above the forest,
        to have a clear view of the clearcutting.*

I stood and watched the tree tops shuffling in horror
        as highlanders tore into their trunks.

38. Truth

I

He left at dawn and settled into a simple
stumble within the song of the doctored
by drink. He liked the violently mangled
roots of the red trees, not the caterpillars
blending into one another like a beating
burial shroud. He longed to clear them
but acquiesced to their mourning mass.
When he paused for water, he noticed
   two leaves waving to him
from the bottom of what he considered
   the world's widest tree trunk.

II

While returning home by canoe, the sky
welcomed eagles, rams, swans and lions.
One constellation returned him to the Irish
grandmother he had never met, had only
seen in two black and white photos. He'd
never heard the lilting brogue of her voice
but had visited her grave. It was crawling
with bugs and the leaves around her waved
as well, or at least that's what he wanted
to believe. He needed these two connected,
even if it meant transforming the plants,
   stars and story.

39. Hollow tree sexting in the Amazon

I

They live within roots, the tones within trunks,
　　　　till freed by the club the crude carver wields.

II

. . . those birthed from a bole, those within trees,
　　　　words freed from and by
　　　　　　　　the hard drive of need.

III

When lust lives alone, it aches. Its tone is the root
　　　　of it all, in want of the sprawl.

IV

. . . mountains of mosquitoes, cliffs and canals,
　　　　omnipotent lust, thrust through them all.

V

But what if one evening, he stumbled, the sender,
weakened by heartache, libido and liquor,
　　　　then woke up to find his bottle and cudgel?
He'd have to uproot, the tree and the tone
　　　　to search for the Hadza and replant it in stone.

40. Sometimes when I swim, I think

of other times
I swam. Once,
in the veins of the world,
in a river
pythonic in purpose,
I was constricted out of my self-pity.

Sometimes when I swim, I am
not, fully, I am drifting
above those
who sank
when they could no longer tread time.

Sometimes when I swim
I tilt my head and listen
with one ear above
and one below
for the voices that supported me
when I descended.

Sometimes when I swim, I whirl
so my head looks like
it is rolling downhill
to be impaled upon a spike
and raised for the sun to savage.

Sometimes when I swim, I bob calmly,
but my legs, you should see my legs.

41. The Kurdish mosquito will fight back

When it paused, I drenched it,
and watched it drag its hind legs
        across the sunset.
If it were my size, it could be said
        I lowered a lake upon it.

                    *

It returned as a night fighter
        to drop tinnitus
into my canals. The ground assault
        bloodied ears.

                    *

I struck it down again at dawn
        in a pure pyrethrin putsch.
I struck it down again at dusk
        in a malathion mist.

                    *

If we ignore the child, gasping
        for breath, the nodding donkeys
who approved of this death,
        we bear blood and blame
for ignoring the plans, to asphyxiate
        Kurds with aerosol cans.

42. Act I

Men drank below on crates and cars to watch a chest
           expand, unfold,
while katabatic currents carved cuneiform into his lungs.
He could not turn and leave them lost, his audience
           of Kurds and kings;
so raised a flask to fan this farce, and danced half lit.
           The chorus sings:
He crawled within the looted heads, to drink, defend,
decry and free, the messengers, the plundered horse,
from looters, ISIS and museum. See the four-winged
           genie flee from Christie's rapist lunacy.

Act II

One shattered arm, half-cleaved, back-curled,
           digs in the earth and bloodies stones.
A spider silhouette expands to slowly shade
                the mouth, the moans.

Act III

Back in the car, a ghastly mess, bloodied in a crimson
           dress, through heat, haze and dust to rest.

Act IV

How many Kurds he waved to then, were deserted,
           left to rage, filmed on fire within a cage?

43. We have bigger problems than caring about wooden fish

Up liquor store road you'll find air conditioner cartons
used as crenellated walls
to divide the haves from
          the could care less. In front of these frail castles
blind jugglers swat
at flies then curse
          the heat and the affluent who look out at the heat.
A few elders on
red plastic lawn-
          chair thrones curse their taxis, the steaming ones
whose promises ruined
their youths, like wives
          do, like children will, like phantom politicians
have. A semi-king sits
on a curb beside a large
          wooden fish that lacks the might to right itself
and find its way back
into the reservoir's
          peace. A fool told me a cat-shaped cloud heaved
it out to feed a
wedding party
          at St. Mary's. I think it jumped from the Sirwan
to warn us of the damming
of rivers and the poisoning
          of water worming south. Not all chemical attacks
come from above.
For the stateless,
a large wooden fish blocking the sidewalk is simply that.

44. You moved like a chariot with chipped wheels

as you tilted and lurched down the mountain
to looted and tagged Assyrian reliefs, calming
yourself by caressing the wind-eroded limbs.
You lumbered home as if your feet were planets
with their own system of orbiting moons, both
drawn differently by gravity. After untying
your shoes, you tapped out shavings of flesh;
your feet, like those on royal messengers, were
being redacted by gales that condemn memory.

Wine was your wheelwright, allowing you to
dance and flow without the chants and guttural
grunts that plagued you; to pause when pissing,
frozen in sculpture — to fall left like a fighter jet
            after unloading its cargo.

I joked about the days a guard would have to drive
to cut a switch in Kurdistan. You said they would
also whip with car antennas and coat hangers.

I thought of us when I saw a motorcycle for double
amputees in Arusha. It had two antennas and shirts
struggling on hangers, flapping like bled corpses.
You told me visions of a man with detachable feet.
He did not fear being wind-whispered away, like
kings carved into crags. He could run when others
ran out of time, sticks and patience. He could flee
the gusts of sarin sent to cripple him differently.

45. Orbs terrify me now

Through a mid-August haze he watched the cockroach-contoured
mountains resting beside others that looked like rotten turtles
with cracked shells; both were struggling to right themselves
like the passenger reclining in the back of the truck pushing down
       through Kurdistan.

We passed power lines, limp and swaying like the dangling necks
of goat roadkill carried by children along the shoulder, and red
Hyundai trucks carrying whatever doesn't need refrigeration,
       and the weight of more that does.

I returned to the rocks all day, and the cemeteries resting beneath
their syphilitic peaks, to the blanched tombstones and their blenched
ecosystems as worn as the panhandler's palms in Hawler.

On the outskirts of Halabja, a piebald cow drinking from a metal
drum raised its head and acknowledged us. We had seen pictures
of its family and owners an hour before at the memorial. Their legs

and bodies bloated from breathing mustard gas. Some looked like
giant balloon animals slowly deflating, while the legs of others
had stiffened into broken compass needles pointing in all directions.

       At dusk we found a post-modern monument to mourning.
A cemetery of orbs, circular sculptures and fixed Pythagorean sails.
A triangle was a limb, an arm, a knee or elbow. Orbs were terrifying
to address; they were the bubbles within foam within mouths within
       children.

46. "Baath's Members are not Allowed to Enter"

I

In Kurdish, Arabic and English: *A prayer for the 24 bodies*
in this grave. These are some of the victims of that ruthless
attack by chemical weapon on the city of Halabja by Saddam's
regime on 16 March 1988 May God bless them. The next
monument is worded the same for 1500 bodies. The next 440 . . .

II

There was a white statue of a woman looking up to the sky.
At Khwa, asking . . . ? At Gas, falling . . . ? She had unchiselled
arms and two large hands resting upon her chest. Someone
held her back? Why? Her blurred face looked like a skull
pressed against a bed sheet on a clothesline. She stood
near the first healthy tree I had seen in Halabja, guarding
                her children's tombstones. They covered acres.

III

Abandoned by the others to scour the ground, I spotted
a radiant green toy gun. I spun and generated a miniature
cyclone of sand while scanning the city and its mountains.
Only here, ten feet in front of me, was this shade of green.
I wanted to find the child who left it. Were you defending
your family from what fell? Did you have a brother or sister?
A cow? Did I walk past you in the memorial? Did you cry
                when you learned you can't shoot gas?

47. A bastardized tombstone for a bastard

If there was a God, good god would I kill,
K—D—, the lecher with whoremonger's
sighs. Just you, only you, would be my
heart's fill. I'm weathered not weaker, I
will fulfill my dagger's desire to sever
your ties. If there was a God, good god
would I kill. Here's one cabaret, one drink
and one pill, one low burlesque lunge to
widen what cries. Just one, only one,
would be my heart's fill. Your colourful
flag will flutter and trill while watching me
carve with cartographer's eyes. If there
was a God, good god would I kill. To
whom should I post it? Those in your will?
The shaft that has set and will no longer
rise. One cold pork pie prick, on whose
windowsill? But sadly, so sadly, how can
I spill your blood
              below brazen celestial lies?
    If there was a God, god would I kill.
    If there was repentance, you'd be my
                    heart's fill.
But what if your murder, it opens my eyes,
and what's left of my mother and morality
dies? But what if I do, good god, if I kill?
How many more like you
                    would be
                        my heart's fill?

48. The saddest toilet

The saddest toilet
sulks in the sun.
Its yellow doors,
white walls
and cinder blocks
slump forlornly
in a field
behind
a god-forgotten
truckstop.
Its corrugated cap
cants to the right
as the wind's palm
thrums on loose hinges
so they trill
like tanbur strings.
After I returned
to my taxi
to rub
little trees
under my nose,
I looked
back
at its silhouette
and wondered:
Did Noah
or Jonah
know a smell like that?

49. Lance the losh and the pastor

Lance's tongue is sick
so the fish sing
to mock his blathering;
the swish of his strainer,
the strike of his chisel.
Wind burn, ice burn, drop
his line to hell.
Fleshed fish, dried fish, nudge
the pressure crack; fold a mausoleum
on his arthritic back.
A congregation hovers,
his old god
rests, as the current passes judgment
on what undertows suggest.
The ministry is ill.
Lord let the bell ring
to mock their blubbering;
the swash of the cassock,
the lustre of the cross,
naves burn, aisles burn, snow
melts into moss.
Warped christ, chipped christ, let
his income wane; counterfeit collection plates
cast and catch the same.
A congregation wonders,
His long reach
numbs, as the damaged and deceived
dig new graves beside their mums.

50. You step over empty Smirnoff bottles poking through the snow

like the first buds of spring, as cracks in the ice warn:
no cargo will come until the shoreline is torn. You enter
below a small light bulb, white budded cross and cruel
Latin: *Evangelizare pauperibus misit me**. Who is poor?
While listening to the wind die, you peer out through
stained glass windows that bleed, cool and warm the land.
You lied to nuns to hunt alone, and found a sacred text
       hidden behind the altar:

Asset Protection Insurance Exchange, ask:
Are you alone in the church today? If so, please ensure:
    1. *No combustible material is left lying around.*
    2. *All flammable liquids, such as gasoline, candle oil*
       or paint thinner, are locked away.
    3. *All valuables are locked away.*
    4. *No unauthorized person is left in the church.*
    5. *Garbage cans are locked away.*
    6. *All doors and windows are securely locked.*
Spend five minutes; save our Church!

In the church basement there are limbless shepherds,
an organ, a broken Favourite Box No. 36 cast iron stove,
damaged pews, a cracked Mary, a broken baby Jesus
and an earless donkey staring at Joseph. It looks like
the Mackenzie broke here first, tore through the hull
of this dollhouse of worship, a warship, unanchored
and ready to drift away with the same river that helped
its captains before time and gravity pulled them under.

51. Émile Petitot, the renowned ethnologist, was a cunt

I call by the compound name of Dene-Dindjie . . . the head elongated, pointed towards the base, unduly raised above. Its greatest breadth is at the cheekbones . . . the forehead is passably high, but it is tapering, conical, depressed towards the temples . . . the arch of the eyebrow is clear cut, but very high and strong marked . . . it shows a large eye, black, ardent and shining with a snake-like lustre . . . the nose is generally aquiline . . . their mouth is wide . . . the chin is pointed, peaked in some, retreating in others . . . their flesh is not soft like that of Europeans, but firm, hard and stiff . . . there are among them neither humpbacks, lame, nor frail and rickety beings, so common in our communities of refined civilization . . . a bilio-limphatic temperament had rendered them liars, disdainful, ignorant, dirty, improvident, without the least real affection, without gratitude, not much given to hospitality, greedy, hard towards women, the old and the weak, blind and over-indulgent towards their children, cowards, idle, dastards, unreflecting, selfish and cheats . . . his was their lot in common with all savages; this was the result of their isolated life, of their total want of education . . . in fact, almost the whole number of the Den-Dindjie is Christian or Catholic . . . they are incapable of appreciating the beauty of a work of art and like all savages, are very sensitive to music . . . they have one rhythm for love; another for war and magic; a third for play; a fourth for dancing and a fifth for mourning and sorrow . . . all these songs are in the minor mode, like the Greek hymns . . . the Dene-Dindjie have accepted and still bear the yoke of the Gospel . . . in the designs, which His wisdom proposes, against which theories and opinions vainly struggle.

52. Dead rabbits

Heaps of dead rabbits were bundled, like old
      slippers in a wooden crate,
still wearing their wire scarves and a new coat
      of hoarfrost.
Their cloudy eyes lingered behind icicled
      prison bar lashes
awaiting sunlight to unstitch so they could
      flutter and flirt
with the hordes of snowflake suitors descending.

When the moon is up, and the twig
      and marten say
          jump,
                vault we must.
Up and into a mélange
              of twitching animals.

While the Ski-Doos idled, Wilfred showed me
how to make hanging snares with woodchips.
But when his axe reflected our misaligned
headlights into the treetops,
                I began to think
of my last jump. What demon will pursue
me into the woods? Whose hand will plant
the twig and tie the wire? Will I struggle,
or just gaze up at the stars that blink back
      like the eyes of noosed rabbits,
opening and closing, opening then closing.

53. Not everything you love will float, the bundled

                                 dolls,
their nestled necks and idle throats. The eddies
                          of eyes,
the whirlpools of limbs, the torsos resting on riverbeds
                       again.
A wolf and a dog, the heft of their lust, will jostle
                      with you
and the lumber you trust. Waterlogged dresses,
                   fences and fawns,
like gas cans of liquor will bob and be gone. Roses
                 on red caps,
a child's warning beacon, will guide the unstable
                away from the deacon.

II

Your houses are older, swollen and sicker,
betrayed by the breakup, the spore and the banker.
What were you offered, what form of grace,
for carving their lies into lines on your face?
        (She looks like a paddle to the agent above,
        as helicopter ripples disperse all you love.
        She sways and careens, face down and weighted
        in a dress of light green, the shoes that she hated.)
Come whitefish. Come losh. Return to my hook
with a rosary of eyes from the children they took.
Come question the weight of what Oblate's began;
        maker, river, heave back what you can.

54. You can't chisel a tombstone with a carrot, or dig

the burial pit with a sand bucket; the items I kicked
when walking to the wake. Nothing is permanent.
Not frost. Not family. A small excavator is crawling
to church. Its death knell is echoing off the ramparts.
Clang.

Headlights, flashlights and cigarette butts, light
this darkness, as the wind and breath of prayers
and jokes mingle around the rabbit hole beginnings
beneath portable flood lights.   *Clang.*
Shadowed faces look like emerging stones resting
above grave depression chests. All are half frozen.

It was no warmer inside Our Lady, ornamented
with life collected from the vegetation.   *Clang.*
So much lifeblood drained from plants to praise.

When the chill of the pews encircles and entombs
your thighs, you turn to Mackenzie *Clang*
to watch the tip of a freshly lit cigarette transform
into an altarlight. It just makes it through the closing
doors before plunging to the floor. When they began,

I closed my eyes to listen to a community use caribou
to eulogize the son they lost. The hide had been dried
and stretched so they could drum and sing for an end
to the perma-pain and perma-faith that has frozen
too many above and below the ground.   *Clang.*

55. Being stuck in a tree is tiring, but the lights . . .

It is one thing to be driven
and baited by a sky
throbbing like mechanized matter,
it is another to be mocked
and upended by the Sahtu's
cloudscapes,
his mangled finger
stippled the same scarlet arcs
and patches
upon the trail he broke,
that dusk would turn and trim.
Did the sky cleave itself open
to unite its pulse
to the battered finger?
Are the patches above
in honour of the patches below?
He knew what he mumbled
would be torn and sky-stretched
into something calming.
In the old movies he watched
as a child, the mist and myth
sent from your lungs
would spiral in upon itself
to nurture you. But in reality,
he was trying to hold his breath.
He feared losing the air that supported
the reds and blues pulsing beneath
the snow on his arm.

56. Wind is what it turns you into

As the wind wails and winds in from the Caspian,
unhinging balcony doors, I watch this tempest
heaving yours.
Bricks become bittern,
jig into eagles, shingles atop dead souls
arch and spiral.

*

A great-grandmother scrambles to shelter her princess,
surrenders her body to strengthen the carriage.
The plant pots that plummet, the dirt clumps that follow
aren't red kites and black kites,
a snowcock or swallow.
How beautiful the bird, angelic, divine,
until it cuts canopy
until it cuts spine.
Wind, water and wheel, most fled you all
but I paused to reflect in a prismatic spill,
then an oriel's echo of the scarf round my throat
let me watch as it levelled like blood pouring out.
I cursed all I dodged, I cursed death's debris
and fled from the shiplap. But the Caspian Sea
and the torn free from ledge
upended my legs and their locomotive pledge.
I hacked near the Ferris wheel,
spewed where few lay,
then paraded down the boulevard like a drunk tank in May.

57. Skulls and all they offer

After the viewing he would never walk without a small
metal pipe hidden in his right sleeve. He held it like a
broken crucifix, striking his legs with it when they began
to cramp. It made him braver when the howls began
      to circle.

Across the nose! You must strike with all your might —
across the nose until you kill it . . . only the rabid attack.
Late one evening an elder told him about a wolf
that had entered a cabin and attacked a woman asleep
      on her couch. It tore into her skull.

He thought of her two years later, while alone in Baku's
old city, staring at a statue of the poet Vahid's head.
Large slabs of his scalp had been cut out, unveiling
a macabre mess of characters trying to barge back
      into the plotline.

It was his eyes, not the allegory, that held him.
Did she possess these when the wolf's teeth entered?
Did he have that look when he was alone on the frozen
Mackenzie as bark-howls arrived from the Ramparts?
      Did the wolf own such eyes before it fell?

How long does it take our threatened eyes to transform
and terrorize? Will I end up under the ice, on a table,
as another's food or inspiration? River, doctor, wolf,
      sculptor, feed off my flesh, honour my eyes.

58. On the tenth of May, when the city flowered, we weaved

through traffic and transit bus barriers to Winter Park, below
balloons that bobbed and swayed like an army of colossal
squids' eyes. The noise would have been dreadful without
the Turkish Supersleep acquired from a kiosk and consumed
along the way. As we walked, our bloodstreams warned:
>> You too should be tethered.

After dodging the tin-like trills of a young boy's tar, I pointed
to the synagogue for Mountain Jews, closed one eye and placed
my fingertips over its windows. After the pills took hold,
we did as well, hauling down two of the ubiquitous balloons
>> adorned with Heyday's malignant mug.

Smiling like toddlers with their first balloons, we released them,
navigated floral sinuosities to the park's northern edge where I
>> raised my left palm to support the European Synagogue.
We steered away from the sermonizers who spoke of this land's

partitioning and how those younger than us were being conned
and carted to jail by cudgel-clad degenerates during the election.
Weeks later, deflated, I walked the old Jewish quarter being sold
by the square metre, to find the shifted Molokans and Armenians.

The dead possess no peace here. Eyes, far and wide, are in both
the sky and subsoil we compress, looking for remains to unearth
and redact. After the pills thinned, one was out, while the other
bobbed through the city looking for something to ground him,
>> heave down or consume.

59. From the Azeri world of the child and young creative palace

A tank is not a summer car,
the sun is not a golden ball, resting
like an air balloon;
there is nothing new in your art of nothing true.

A tree is not an ice cream cone,
a fighter's arms aren't tentacles, offering
doves to garish rays;
there is nothing new in your art of nothing true.

Your axle does not touch the tank,
where crullers turn as track and tire, paltry
pastries off to war.
There is nothing new in your art of nothing true.

Why are your birds and railway spikes,
broken arms or butchered legs, melting
into waxen plash?
There is nothing new in your art of nothing true.

It takes no effort to debunk,
when the barrel is a trunk, nothing
but manned elephant;
there is nothing new in your art of nothing true.

Your colours, cars, cats and fire,
fail to uplift or inspire;
you'll age into nothing new in your land of nothing true.

60. I am loosening on a train to Tbilisi with Irakli

The rush and roll
of the perpetually derailing train
is half buggery, half bowery waltz.
We will take air, great air, two stories or more
above this aquarium track sewerage system
that drives through wastewater
and the vomited gristle
of suicidal
cows.

Each screw
sings of its re-
turning, the circling back
into its warbling world being razed to the ground.
When the train slows, you hear them again,
the chairs and coaches, loosening
and growing.

They will fall
out, like the rest of us,
grounded and graceless
but a little rusty. When we arrive,
customs will mingle as families try to crawl
in, under and over, the oscillating arms
and legs of those who hate
society's cramp-
ons and cut
spikes.

61. Heartened by hops, their spirits and song

the hangman and hung men of the cast iron choir
watched me through dimmed eyes, sun damaged
and fading, like portraits on tombstones,

                              staring as well.

(They swig and they sing to a fictitious king.)

Tree trunks of marble were both bench and table,
grape vodka bottles lay shattered on graves
where sweetness was missing, where a courtyard
was stolen, by the weeds of demise whose stems

                              raised the dead.

(They swig and they call for a fortified wall.)

Pamphlets are drifting like leaves through the walkways
misleading those waltzing in thinking it's fall.
The wind has grown bitter, purely pernicious,
dismantling the gated, one gait at a time.

(They swig and they weep, then sway half-asleep.)

My voice was unwelcome, bruised by the bourbon
that opened the alley then curved it in curse.
For being too upright, aseptic and uptight,
I was run out while finding a plot for my verse.

(I offer my grave men, this song as your hearse.)

62. Some cornfields look like concentration camps

Everything will ashen. Blanched photographs
are being gathered, burned and offered
windward. Tassels and ears,
hermaphrodites and bisexuals
are being stripped
and unhusked.
The acreage has weakened, the soil
has loosened. Stalk rot and root rot
have forced some to summon great winds
to bowl back this aggressiveness.
They planted barbed wire on cracked
concrete poles
hoping common rust and smut
would not topple them; sacrificial
anodes won't be enough.
Field after field
are clambering out of the camps,
drying and dying.
The sun and the rain will dehydrate and drown,
as bulwarks of leaf blight
battle and fade. Adventurous roots
will be uprooted and slit.
You are here. Stalk and spine.
Torn silk and husk.
A field of indictments.
Corn corpses will be dishonoured
and forgotten, unless the wind-stung and soilless
are filmed, harvested or burnt.

63. Theatre of the absurcumcised I

Just one sip and I would have been anesthetized
like his father, with eyes glazed and gazing two
centuries beyond the festivities. His colleagues,
a group of young men behind the women's hut
guzzling blood from mud masonry, smiled as I
        walked my father to the outhouse.

I stood tall outside the toilet. Framed by Meru,
its blue sky and lush slopes, I tried to look regal
and menacing. But before returning to our seats,
I was given a bowl of cow's blood that reddened
my lips and chin like I had applied lipstick while
battling a lion, or like when aunts transformed
my baby cheeks into cave paintings; although
the blood's smell didn't need to be cleansed
        with rank saliva from musty mouths.

Hundreds of Maasai sat on the surrounding hills
watching this unfold. The opera box dug into it
transported me back to the Bolshoi. I wanted
to yell *bravo* to see if the young men would stop
the ceremony and bow. It was a day of costumes,
consumption and song; a fenced-in orchestra pit
sent incidental moos and bleats for atmosphere.

I declined to return for Act II. He did not need
a mzungu with a camera while his arms and legs
were being restrained, his flesh cut and tossed.

64. Theatre of the absurcumcised II

We left the uncircumcised boy to dance
and sing and jump while others danced
and threatened his character in song.
His father bounced to the main entrance,
his stash bottle necklace bounding
from forehead to chest, covering his face in a cloud
of tobacco as he greeted those bringing alcohol
and goats, cows and more alcohol,
until their huts bulged like their bellies.
Drunk fathers and drunk brothers, with lips
reddened by bowls of blood,
waved goodbye to us
and all the others who fled mid-afternoon.
My bobblehead banged and bled
as we descended the ridge, tilting
as crevice after crevice
attempted to consume our car.
Overdressed toddlers approached us and fled
when I lowered my tinted window
to reveal my true colours.
I could hear my Maasai friends singing and laughing
when I left the car to rest beneath a tree.
Its branches were being used like clotheslines
to dry hides — one looked like a burnt and bloodied flag,
another, the shirt of a suicide bomber.

Tomorrow, that poor boy's foreskin might be here,
pegged and waving in the wind.

65. To be given gifts for something other than silence

        and coerced consent, was never your world.
Toys and rags were used to redress and cleanse
        what's left of him from off of you.
While sitting amongst the shadows cast by broken
glass on cinder blocks that looked like the teeth
        that just tore you, did you wonder

if the mould maker, kiln operator and assembler
had known how their toys were used, would they
have hidden a knife in the tiny trunk of the car
or a cyanide pill in the pupil on the train's face?
The men who poured the concrete that was piled
in the abandoned lot, what would they do to him
if they knew what happened to you within the walls
        of their unfinished shell.

You were disposable once unboxed and assembled,
with no concern for your condition. You learned
limbs can be scratched and bent and manipulated
when forced. Hands, like fathers, can be twisted,
clothing torn; talking dolls can be muted like TVs.

When I walked you to school, I had three daggers
hidden in my coat to protect you from the flagitious
who wanted you disassembled, incinerated, coffined.
They would have thrown you in a ditch for being
twenty years shy of vintage. For not mimicking
        mint in box, they wanted you dead and buried.

66. Even the sound of popcorn has been taken

Your confessional clothes were soiled
inside and out
from squatting in the bathroom stall.
Some would have wept.
Some would have wailed.
But you curled in the bathroom
and calmed,
knowing the orphanage and school
would never search where it stinks.
Not one note made it through
your curled-cup mute fingers
when you were hacking
and heaving out
the memory of your father's filth.
Beautiful though, isn't it?
How the light slithers sockless
down the wall,
like the spiders and centipedes
you've befriended.
There are too many like you
in the cribs at the bad place,
oscillating like the warming kernels
in Baraa's new popcorn machine.
When I was your age, I rushed to the sound
you flee.
Is it the pop, or how the kernel jolts
as if awakening from a nightmare,
that makes you run away?

67. Prescribed fires — burn them burn them burn them

The thrown
brick strikes

back. The
school wall

holds back.
The barbed

wire cuts
back. The

hurt hand
fights back.

The base
beast bears

down. An
old man

drives in.
A small

child lights
        fires.
Some fires
must catch.

68. Every elephant has been hung from a tree

shot with fireworks and tagged by graffiti
artists at war with the river, rain and all
          the weight water carries to nudge.

When a gin bottle clips and clinks off rocks,
a few birds might resolve to walk toward
the perceived courtship. But when your legs
are bound and the scale of your wings is off,
you sit and stare at a life drawing to a close.

Lions slowly expire, like anesthetized elders,
while birth and learning, courtship and kill,
no longer curve or stretch the necks of others
          hidden amongst the vegetation.

The oddities who straggle through this valley,
weighted and wobbling, offer the cargo
of their conscience to the forest to awaken
the weary. For there are also those lusting
behind the same trees that support the men
they intend to crush. What of the cubs, colts,
chicks, infants, calves and pods of hatchlings?

When you return to Berlin and Brussels to laugh
with those who funded your hunt, will you show
them all the photos of the feast? Will you describe
how you made some families watch as you broke
the skeleton of both artist and artwork to pieces?

69. Boreholes

I

In this world atop boreholes
they tilt water tables, as the rain within children
begins tilting as well.
When wastewater swaggers, the cried echo craters
for the curled heave of water
needs somewhere to set.

II

A man in a suit enters an office with a briefcase
he borrowed containing paperwork he helped
forge. He fumbles with the latch. He puts
documents on the table. One document is the
chemical analysis of his school's new borehole.
He bribed the men in the lab to alter the
findings. He looks out the window as he places
another bribe on another desk. He closes the
briefcase. He practised how to do this without
looking down, for this is not the time to look
down. Confident men stare out windows. 1400
children will be poisoned by confident men.

Today, I am admiring the bay and how easily
they could be erased here. The seals bored holes
wide enough for corpses to be lowered. Let
the portly pricks drown in unpotable water.

70. Goodbye Zanzibar Penal Code 1934

I

god bless your dress, not the penal code
decrying it
god bless your dress, not the crucifix
adorning it

god bless your dress, not the chastener
renouncing it
god bless your dress, not the tuck and tape
demeaning in it

II

I fear for your home, and the enmity
exhausting it
I've seen barleycorn, and the barely born
unfed in it

I fear for your blood, and the DSH
releasing it
I fear what's to come, the taskforce sent
to bottle it.

III

If he distorts might, if he distorts melody,
he'll hoist and he'll hang your innocents faithfully.

71. The raft of the Toyota Tacoma

There were two drummers, young men,
one sitting with his back to the cab,
the second curled against an off-white
tailgate taped and bungee-corded shut;
five silver sticker signallers performed

as well. Four trumpeters aimed their horn
bells at the cargo bed to deflect their joy
up through the valley to quiet the belly-
        aching vespers volleyed down.

Six trombonists faced one another, three
a side, their slides raised skyward to create
an arbour of brass and nickel, glimmering
        with glacial abundance.
(Out of the passenger window, a drunken
head and right arm flapped like fish tied
to the side view mirror, market bound.)

After they disappeared, I noticed two
blonde JWs in khaki pants struggling
as the wind tore at *The Watchtower*
and *Awake!* As I awaited the ensemble's
crescendo, hoping its wave would crest
and cleanse the streets of these two-toned
evangelicals struggling to look righteous,
I found a renewed faith and comfort
in knowing nature despised them as well.

72. Lift is loyalty

Throughout the long rains the watering hole's washrooms
        overflow.
Unwilling to drink elsewhere, regulars never wear new shoes
        or sandals
or place their groceries and children on the ground. You learn
which tables have pedestal bases so you can rest your feet
        above the urine line.

It arrives swiftly, like our laughter and applause, as it shunts
        a few back onto the street.
We have accepted what is enlarging a few feet below our fries
        and beer,
the cigarette butts that resemble hotels in old tsunami footage
and capsized cockroaches floating by like unmanned longships.

When the power is out, we sit and talk to the rhythm of the rain
pounding the tin roof as chair after empty lawn chair inches
toward the highway entrance to greet those pouring out of dala
dalas. Some dance and stomp in the rain to temper their time.
        We are all aware of our numbered days

as we watch soul after sole rotting, never discussing what dark
        patches in urine
foretells. We pollute ourselves while believing the waste we've
        given rise to
is our way of honouring the battle. What inspires this flowing
        celebration is a desire
to demonstrate we can still create something that moves people.

73. Karl Schmidt's ghost walks Baraa

4:00am Don't tread upon the limners left upon the dirt paths, descend and navigate rocks, holes, streams, shin high crops, irrigation ditches and one river. 4:30am Weighted by heat or venom, your vision will blur until plastics metamorphose into boomslang. 6:30am Plastic bags blown into cornfields will enwrap the husks like tutus. A troupe of ballerinas will dance while larger bags caught and rustling in another field's cabbage create the din of applause. 7:00am Fill Konyage bottles with river water, shake and overturn the antithetical snow globe, watch the particles dance and dart like comets. 5:30pm Marvel at Meru reflected in the irrigation ditch as a gum wrapper plane covered in ants crashes into its peak. 6:30pm Run with the children towing chicken box kites, show them the bottle caps ferrying beetles to the valley below, where shoe, bag and blouse waltz and whirl into hydro dams. 8:30pm Laugh with the young boy frantically waving a stick at the punctured tire fleeing down the cowpath. 9:00pm Stop and wave to everyone. Never worry about your standing in the community, bend to it. Ask them not to clean the rivers and paths of Baraa. Capitulate to the carnival of clutter and let the children make toys from all at their feet. 4:30am Violent nausea, eyes bleeding, dreams of an undivided anal plate.

74. Four reasons you don't need long grass for nightmares

In the morning you were told
the bark, the bray and snort
that altered your dreams
were zebras being possessed
        and unweighted.

        *

Grass does not have to be long
to cloak the predators
that move as gracefully
        as variegated sky.

        *

It is not the whole of creation,
but a mesmerizing flow
of your memories, galloping
and surging. Whatever rests
behind your eyes, it is, or can be.

        *

When moonlight strikes verdureless
blades, you feel uneasy about your
struggle for order. What would this
order resemble? How would you
live within it? Who would join you?

75. He said, "Dik-diks never remarry, like christians."

the little ones
look up to me
the christian ones
not yet alone

they live in fear
the little ones
soon to be torn
from horn to tail

by everything
above the grass
by everything
that winds within

sun come blanch
wind come take
the bones of all
the little ones

see my fingers
worried ones
signum crucis
now be done
go live in fear
as christian ones
as christian ones
with simple fears

76. Chase whatever you can make float

       Retrenching never looked so adorable;
the piglet's shuffle and waddled rebuke to all
the long and short-legged aggressors, snorting
like anesthetized academics, bloated, beard
and all. The wobble in Earth's rotation is far
less amusing than a piglet's ass chasing flecks
freed by trampling. The dry season is a dream
mill, grinding blades of grass to be chased
like bubbles blown through plastic wands.

       I was reawakened by the military
march of forks, and the scrambling of glasses
across a tray like passengers on an overturning
cruise ship. Across the road I saw the winsome
gait of youth fading. Penniless, they skulked
in the shadows, still selling soap in unlabelled
wine bottles at 10pm. These semi-sounders
in torn green sweaters stirred up clouds of dust
particles then paused to watch them waltzing
       within a circus of hurdling high beams.
After a few minutes they left for their valley
of fragmented infancy, where predators wait,
drinking from tin cups, boiling banana pulp.

There are no walls enclosing Tarangire, so let
the children from the villages move in. Harm
will come, as it always does, but at least they
will be able to chase the airborne by sunlight.

77. After the cackle enters and the wrestling within

and with, the sheets subsides, there is still time
to deceive yourself into believing mosquito nets
aren't the wrong form of firewall. If you drawer
the match and candle that would topple the tent
in seconds, you unwelcome the whine and whoop
that wants the canvas to take, and their food
      to rush out, grilled and flailing.

All fear should be hidden from the cub's eyes
that would moisten like their lips when reflecting
the flames. When your flashlight falls to the floor,
freeing the batteries to scuttle like cockroaches
      below the bed, leave them.
Bin the elephant whistle. It only beckons minors
dressed in tourist shop robes who are studying
for their entrance exams. They are not morans
who will dash toward the burning tent to wield
uncharmed textbook elongos and disposable pen
      spears.

Barks, brays and snorts, stumbling and humming,
roars and growls; these noises fade. The net is not
on fire, the tent is not ablaze. Rest and wait upon
these well-grazed grasslands. Nothing will burn
blue and green tonight, and when you awake, half
on the floor, enwrapped in a spider's web of rayon,
celebrate your thumping heart and skin, still fresh
      and whole.

78. She lifted his nostrils above the waterline

while he slept. Never abandoning him
to the struggles below. But it saddens me
when he burrows and yawns, for his meat
will be consumed, his canines and incisors
pulled and carved into figurines. He sleeps,
unaware that a few airplanes away there lies
an industry that dressed his ancestors in tutus
to pirouette until they fainted. Then Milton
broke his elders by demanding they engorge
themselves on plastic marbles while having
their asses pounded.

The children who slept with soft, plush
versions of you are now the evangelicals
and volunteers, arriving monthly to poach
and plunder other types of schools.

But don't blame the peasants who hunt, eat
and trade your body. They love their babies
as well. It is the rich who have exploited
your pods for years. Look at your cousin
overturned in the river, being nudged home
by an alligator, blanched belly coated in flies;
at least he is free from them. His body will
never become a silicone mould for a nightlight.
He will never have a lightbulb forced down
his throat so others can drift safely to sleep,
like infants should. Like you before me now.

79. Ancient alphabets walk the Serengeti

From a distance, the elephants of the Serengeti
look like families and their baggage, gliding
on an autowalk from one border to another.
Others look like tumbling clouds comprised
of that bitter, vengeful hate, growing in me
for cloth and country; hidden for years, it has
        now solidified into a herd of madness.

There is a commune of consumptives shaking
behind the volcanic rock where jaguars rest,
hacking and heaving black phlegm into
mammoth shadows. An author is hiding
within them after committing career suicide.
He has to place his books within the tires
of plane wrecks and then free them to bounce
        and bound away like gazelles.

Is the Serengeti a landing pad or dumping
ground? Are rocks unfinished monoliths?
Am I descended from what lives and walks
        or from what was discarded here?

I watched elephants evolve into Asomtavruli
script. I saw Lasi and Pari guarding their calves.
I had hoped the answers to life were hidden
within parable and pachyderma. But when
confronted, we both paused and huffed until
one moved on and the other sat down, puzzled.

80. Tanzanite mining is government-sanctioned racism and torture

The hands of miners
are crippled
            and shaking.
The hands of owners
are uncut and agile.

The blue and violet
mined, is the blue
and violet
            hidden
by tinted window
shirts and pigment.

You descend for your
children
            and pray
that being in the black
is of value. For black
is a journey down,
            rarely up
                        and out.
It is the ink on your
            bank statement,
the lung shadow
            on your X-ray.

It is birth and death.
            Blocks B and D.

81. The small planes sent to count elephant herds

are circumcising Meru. They are the hum and haw
       of the gossiping grasslands in the sky
that will be silenced as the political skyscape shifts.
More clouds will be discharged to hide mountains,
fog will nestle villages. Everything will be covered
except the president's mouth and the ears that obey.

I scanned the path for Kalahari Ferraris and carried
cigarettes to grind into scorpion bites. The beaten
paths and fields around her house were never empty.
Millions of eyes watched. Their soldiery was slowly
advancing through tunnels constructed by their prey.
Admiral adders and colonel cobras expanded into
the gasp and gospel of my mumbled mania. I returned
to sit and stare at the chasm beneath my front door.
I lit candles to herald the hideous into metal pots after
adding an inch of water. I must draw the monsters up
and over and down. I coated everything in repellants,
to make my fear flammable. At 2am the pickled cobra
in the storage room beside my bed began unscrewing
the lid while the murdered woman thrown in a field
with her eyes sewn shut materialized; drowning men
in overturned helicopters called for help as my pillow
deflated like the breath of a student lifted into a tree
by a jaguar. I rattled matches to ward off intruders.
I fled to her guest house in hopes of dissipating the fog
slithering through the valleys below. But everything
is connected. It had followed me. Just another match . . .

82. https://www.youtube.com/watch?v=SPcZ8Zm958M

There are black panthers below Meru, driven out of their
country by the bastards behind every bush in the eighth
congressional district. From Boot Heel to Lead Belt,
      they were driven far, driven out

until the BPP of the beleaguered woods lowered their fists
      to feed and clothe a village.
Theirs was never a lost world, but one twisted by the time
      and tint of the topographer's thumb.

There are black panthers encircling their cubs with walls
and water, far from the treachery of HUAC and the pigs
who thought Geronimo did not live for the service of all.
In their classroom's greater collage, none are anchored.
      What lives, lives to liberate.

At the end of their dirt road riddled with potvalleys sits
a farm surrounded by barbed wire. Its chimneys send up
clouds of smoke that resemble rationed cotton balls, little
puffs of poverty that return me to the camps in Poland
run by white supremacists, identical to those still hunting
      black (insert anything) today.

We are a shallow people, who never learn to rage against
the right enemies. They are many, growing, and travelling
      at the speed of light in neocolonial cables.
But there are none to fear on this road. No monstrosities.
      Never were. Never will be.

83. Crawl

Upon the escarpment side of the road, on the edge
of the Great Rift Valley, upon
gravel and shards of glass
pop tabs and crushed cans, upon
perpetual scrap, the flaky and friable
world of the hard shoulder.
Upon the debris of chicken lost. Upon
wind born migrations of filaments
and screw thread contacts.
Upon all the remnants of collisions and windshield wiper
arms bent into *vs*
for the vainglorious who snapped
photos from the tourist bus. Upon torn
illustrations of Christ, freed from the candle
by radiant heat. Upon
labyrinths of cigarette butts, sparkwheels and hoods.
Upon everything jettisoned by them
he crawled, pulled and dragged
his body toward the petrol station. All
before him and some after shone softly
in the sunlight and exhaust fume haze.
Some flashed like little Christmas lights
after they nicked and cut those legs entwined
like braided hair. I dreamt that he
was an ornament, crawling
back to the tree. Just a head, shoulders and arms
finding his way home.
To be hung. To be left hanging.

THE

YELLOW

ROOM

84. It took one room in the KGM to end decades of yellow

It was the colour of sunflowers
on our cooking oil bottles. It was the colour
of the leotard, tutu and pointe shoes. It meant
nature and art and logical loss.

It protested time unfolding.
It was royal in a living room painted to protect
his mother from the tawny tint he'd seen on his
grandmother's abandoned skin.

It rose from the sheet music
performed by his brother and the bloated
and worn books dried in the sun
so more books could be illuminated at night
by its slithering campfire cousins.

It was within the wood trimming
behind judges at international tribunals, on string
bracelets above hands held protectively, on hidden
knives he loathed carrying.

It is gone now. It has left all
of Botero's work, Repin's Sadko, *The Colour
of Spring*. It still exists, but to his rods and cones
it is raging and inflamed. At the end of the tunnel
the light is not white and waiting.
It is combative and coming. Not at once. Yellow
erases whites last. If at all.

85. Name: Fillette

If gods exist, they slept her eight seasons,
heard no alarms. Who had the two trumpets,

Age: 2

the hammered steel? Did a schism deafen
you to her pleas, her "no"? For you chose

Favourite Toy: Doll

to ignore the thud and crack of her being
unbodied. What is needed to rouse you?

Best Friend: Her dad

When airpower is only air, what resistance
is there? When lethargy is leveraging law,

Behaviour: A good girl

there is nothing left to wail, but *mommy,
daddy, thank you, ball, bath*, all gone, all . . .

Cause of death: Smashed against a wall

When a childhood is heaved and the wall
doesn't move, no work was done, by gods,
        governments, humanity, none.

86. Irene and Uwamwezi

Did you share the moon, its drag and drift?
Did you share the wind, its folds and force?
Did you share the fields, their slopes and shifts?
Did you share the tree, its hollowed trunk?
Did you share the rain, its wash and weight?
Did you touch the stars, tap on, tap off?
Did you share the sheets, their burst and bloat?

Age:	6 and 7
Relationship:	Sisters
Favourite Doll:	A toy they shared
Favourite Food:	Fresh fruit
Behaviour:	Daddy's girls
Cause of death:	A grenade thrown in their shower

Did you share your songs, their sweep and swing?
Did you share your doubts, then doubt their worth?
Did you share your fears, in whispered code?
Did you share your awe, its jolt and jerk?
Did you share the chill, before the throe?
Did you lose your trust in brain and brawn,
        before their blitz and shrapnel sprawl?

9855 days later:
Did you see them sail to the god of war?
Did you see little Ginny hover and land?
Is the red the same red from shower to soil?
Is the red planet red for we bled their girls first?

87. Ariane, for months now I have seen you on the water's edge

Age:	4
Favourite food:	Cake
Favourite drink:	Milk
Enjoyed:	Singing and dancing
Behaviour:	A neat little girl

You lean on a window ledge that looks like one of the serpents I caught in Lalish. I push you into my house, making the house yours and this dream not mine alone. You go out on the lake in a long canoe to raise money for children whose parents, ramified by rage, partitioned and picked each other off. You sit in the kitchen with your mother and mine and watch my grandmother making the gravy she loves. You will be shown places to hide: under beds, within dresses, in the attic behind the first row of crates, under the front stairs where coats hang and in the drainage pipe, pre-grating, that opens into Lake Ontario. This old version of me, who I can create less and less these days, loved cake, milk, singing and dancing as well. His family would have laughed with yours and showered kisses upon your tiny cheeks. If only you were white. The UN would have come if you were white.

Cause of death: Stabbed in her eyes and head.

88. Red roses for Patrick

They did not need to cut and clear
children; they cannot be harvested
          or replanted,
and those broad blades were not
          born murderous,
but when swung with a tailwind
          torn from a radio's
Public Slaughter Announcement

little ones

dropped.

Like you, in your long striped shirt,
          white socks and shoes,
camping for the camera. I have spent
more hours gazing at your photo,
          your knees, smile and hand,
than any other save the red roses
          above my mother's ashes
that you now rest beneath in my wallet.

Age:	5
Favourite sport:	Riding bicycle
Favourite food:	Chips, meat and eggs
Best friend:	Alliane, his sister
Behaviour:	A quiet, well-behaved boy
Cause of death:	Hacked by machete

89. Romeo is not bleeding alone

Two years after I read with you in Lunenburg, I trudged
through Kigali during the season when rain collapses
onto the city like a weakened overpass, advancing shopping
carts and baby carriages passed banks and the heavily armed
                security guards lining the streets.

Sculptured gorillas hidden beneath a tree's umbrella
                awaited a bus. Others had knuckle-
walked into the roundabout's garden to see their family
                and scan the motorway. Would they
be activated if the terror returned? This was not Arusha.
                It was oncology-ward clean.
Garbage, like conversion therapy pamphlets, was too
                important to be overlooked
or sidestepped. I spent the morning exploring the semi-
                tolerant streets before entering

the yellow room. After I saw the children your fade began.
I lumbered out with a troop of concrete gorillas stomping
on my shoulders. I longed for an end to the enslaved ones,
to enter the volcano range awash in pungent cologne as I
snapped photos in Multi Flash Mode while chest-thumping
in front of silverbacks. I wanted to approach their infants
in a fitful fury to provoke the biting, pounding and tearing
I needed to toughen me. I needed to open myself to: *Milk
and Fanta, chocolate and cake. Milk and Fanta, chocolate
and cake. Milk and Fanta* . . . until all the yellow in me
                fucked off.

HOME

IS

EVERYWHERE

BUT

WHERE

YOU

STAND

90. The waxing crescent was out. I had walked into the lake

to stand waist-deep in rainbow ripples like a semi-aquatic
census monitor — to watch the 35 until the stories and data
of those on it grew tiresome. Turning away from Minden
is easy until you are neck deep and watching the treeline

sway. I could feel the tanks and soldiers nearing. I couldn't
flee for a magnetic boot of muck and milt tethered me.
Like an old Russian television just turned off, the water
was one motionless expanse of forest and Persian green,
            popping and cracking.

I looked up, fearing it would explode, and stayed frozen
for an hour until someone turned the television back on
so I could rewatch myself a decade ago in Kurdistan,
            listening to my colleague's fears.

I entered their stories and closed my eyes to help animate
the purr and click of the tank's wheels and tracks. I stood
up to my neck in dirt as they approached to drive over
my skull, to crack and compress it like a cockroach beneath
            jeering and jackboot.

I was roused by a swarm of dragonflies tapping the lake,
sending messages of concern by Morse code. A mating
couple struck the water with such might that I felt I was
in outer space observing an atomic bomb's detonation.
I lowered myself to mute it and slow my heart. But they
            kept tapping and tapping and tapping.

AMIIKKIQTAINAGAA
(PAULATUK
JOURNAL
FRAGMENTS)

Amiikkiqtainagaa

You can lower your life onto the bay —
        motion mines onto the ice

to open holes to hasten the descent.
Within today's fog, a mischief of rats

is boarding the *Arctic Tern* so they can
welcome the sins barging downward

onto Darnley Bay. I am conducting
this sinking song with the violent air

qunguyugyuumiyuaq

built by those warming our waterways.
        Train after train of our tyrannies

is arriving. That cloud you see above
the Amundsen Gulf is coal smoke

but not rooted in *paula*. Thousands will
end here. The orphan makers, the oven

runners, the widower widowing others
and the death-delighting hell-reachers.

I will douse dawn's palette in petrol,
        burn them to ash on the ice.

unnuaq sinaaqsikangiiyaaqtunga

I am waiting in the middle of Darnley
to confront the arriving. When I see

a sundog, I see three trains and jump
into *Rodger* to listen as ski springs

crash into its hull. Bottles and cans
purl like blinded birds. Satellite dishes,

tires and snowmobile hoods have all
been torn and heaved at the horizon.

iyilangaiqtuaq

I am returning to the shoreline to record
the bay's marginalia while a polar

vortex assaults my eyes, throat and story
lines. What I thought a bag — a running

board, a dog — a tumbling caribou's head.
When I crawl for clarity, it feints

to the left and whirls around to burst in
            and alarm my lungs.

It forces my throat to clog like frozen
pipes — bars entry. I crouch on the old

saraumiillaktuaq

wooden steps of the boarded-up priest's
house. With eyes frozen shut from tears

replacing tears, I tear off my gloves
              and press my palms into

them. My mouth becomes a samovar,
              warming the air within

while the mondegreen murmurs
of the gale tear at my body, trying

qitusuliqtuaq

              to rattle me. It is the same wind
that caused a shipwreck, only to attack

the store made from the wood
of the wreckage. It wants to force me

down to my knees, for me to pretend
I find theogony in its strength, or see

the glistening godlings shimmering
in everything it fells upon me. It wants

to send me onto the sawtooth ice-
splinters so my blood can be freed

qiasunnguliqtuag

to enlarge towards the orphaned lakes
surrounding us. I recover and walk

to find, bury and honour what once
walked and swam beside me before

the ravens can sever and apportion
her little paws into the pelagic pit.

I cover her with stones and the blade
        of a shovel. In late spring

taktuguqsimaakiqtuaq

I hope the land will allow me to cart
        her bones to my mother's ashes.

While searching for her, I saw numen,
dressed in black, peering at me through

a plane's fuselage. They'd posed dolls
in recumbent annunciation. They glared

at me from behind the trees on Northern
Store bags, which were the only trees

for over a hundred kilometres. I saw one
sitting on the skeleton of a snowmobile.

ingitchungiluaqɬuni ingitɬaqtuq

I am done burying her — humming
nervously to the chording of ravens

and power lines dancing together
as a semi-gale flips its sweepings

past a dog in need of enchantment.
            The wind will hold off tonight.

Wooden skids covered in gasoline
must warm the earth for grave digging.

amiimmaniqqamigaa

I am within a grid created by wind,
water, rock, wolves and grizzlies,

looking out my window and imagining
all the cruelties I have seen, coffined

and sinking. But like the garbage here,
I am forced to accept nothing ever goes
underground or gets barged away — but

the semi-scholars who arrive with such
an abundance of baggage they need their
own planes, they will hole up and claim
immunity to all things above and below.

Inuvialuit (Siglit dialect)

Amiikkiqtainagaa — he finally started taking the skin off of it

qunguyugyuumiyuaq — he suddenly had a big smile on his face

unnuaq sinaaqsikangiiyaaqtunga — last night it took me a long
time before I could fall asleep

iyilangaiqtuaq — he cannot easily hide himself anymore

saraumiillaktuaq — he screamed for a little while

qitusuliqtuaq — he suddenly felt like laughing

qiasunnguliqtuag — he suddenly felt like crying

taktuguqsimaakiqtuaq — it is starting to become foggy

ingitchungiluaqłuni ingitłaqtuq — although he didn't want to
sit down, he found himself sitting down

amiimmaniqqamigaa — he has just finished taking the skin off
of it

*Source:
Sallirmiut Inuvialuit Dictionary
Second Edition – Revised and Expanded by Ronald Lowe
Fonds Gustave Guillaume
Universite Laval, Editions Nota Bene
2001 – ISBN 2-89518-072-5

Extended Table of Contents

The Yellow Room

Home is everywhere but where you stand

Amiikkiqtainagaa (Paulatuk journal fragments)

Acknowledgements

I would like to thank everyone at ECW Press for their kindness, generosity and support.

Thank you to my editor, Adam Levin.

I would also like to thank Catherine Graham and Ava Homa for all of their editorial assistance.

My father Colin Woodcock and Nin Schafer, Kevin Kinderplunder and Heather Goof Tom Choo, BJ Soloy. Gaye Facer and Tim Irwin. Michael Stewart and Louise Cochrane. All the McQuades. Kassius, Terry, Savanna, Andy and Millie Green, Jeremy, Chloe, Aaron and Carla Ruben in Paulatuk, Anthon Jensen, John Stiles and Veridiana Toledo. Mitch MacKay and FB, Brendan Monroe, Lukas Cowey. My dear friend Chris Palmer and Tingyu. Dear Aqua — I found and honoured you my friend. With much love to Mama C, Pete O'Neill and everyone at the United African Alliance Community Center and Baraa Primary School, Arusha, Tanzania. The Tanzanian poet Edmond Azaza. The Swahili Art Collective who provided me with a table in the valley to write and watch them paint. Mr. Thomas. My new brother David Chambo. Qat Piki. Siyamand Ali. Andrew 180, Viv and Rachael. Courtney and Barbara Nickerson. Aaron Autut, Cory Kane, Mark Anto, Eduardo Diazgranados, Michael Murphy. Jesse Schaefer, Ed Hoey and the omnipotent Morag, Matt Enticknap, Tim Taylor. The band — Carter Rivet and the Finnish Backpacks.

A very special thank you to Þórarinn Eldjárn for all his words of encouragement and help with my Iceland poems — in remembrance of his son and my friend Kristján.

I am forever grateful to Dilan Dance Company, Toronto, ON Canada, their Artistic Director and Choreographer — the ethnomusicologist and dance scholar, Fethi Karakecili and the dancer Asli Rakkas. Thanks to Romeo Dallaire for his generosity and kind words when we read together in Lunenburg, NS.

For Jordan and all his strength.

Thanks to CUSO International and United for Literacy for not forgetting about Canada's north like far too many have.

A great thank you to my musical collaborator and friend — the brilliant singer songwriter Bill Pritchard — who helped me far more than I can possibly express here. Please check out all of his albums. Thank you as well, Alice Pritchard— for helping us while recording.

To the musicians and composers Steve Kilbey, GB3, Yves Altana. Ellery James Roberts, Ebony Hoorn and everyone involved with LUH, and the brilliant engineer Scott Ralph. My best to Gunther Buskies, Sean Newsham and everyone at Tapete Records.

Thank you Mama C for starting it all off with your beautiful reading of "Crawl."

The Writers Federation of Nova Scotia, the League of Canadian Poets, the Writers' Union of Canada and PEN Canada.

Many of these poems were read at different stages of their development at:

Winnipeg International Festival, Canada
Lunenburg Lit Festival, Canada

Halifax Library Reading Series
Cabot Trail Reading Series
Jahazi Literary and Jazz Festival, Zanzibar, Tanzania
KPF Poetry Festival, Kenya

Some of the poems in various stages of development were
published in the chapbooks — *The Cane, Valley, Boomslang are
hilarious*, and *Chris plays chess*.

I must thank Mihail Chemiakin for letting me use his brilliant
painting for my cover without charging me a cent.

(wmlt) Michele Francis
Please watch: https://www.jackfrancis.ca/videos

Please donate your hair or support the Angel Hair for Kids
program: https://www.acvf.ca/angel-hair-for-kids.

Endnotes
(much longer endnotes for each poem can be found at:
https://farhangbook1.com/)

9. While visiting Vilnius, Lithuania, I tried to find what was
   described in the tourist booklet as a 17 foot tall sculpture of
   Frank Zappa's head. It was the first monument erected to
   him in the world after his death. What they did not point
   out was that the head was only about a foot high standing
   on a 16 foot pole. So I spent the day trying to find a massive
   head while freezing in Lithuania's winter winds.

16. The italicized lines were written by the Russian poet
    Mayakvosky and taken from his poem *About That* (1923).

18. This piece is for my friend Kristján Eldjárn (1972–2002) It
    is also for his father, the Icelandic poet Þórarinn Eldjárn,
    who helped me with this piece and has shown me such
    kindness in the years since Kristján passed.

21. This piece was begun years ago. I used to go to the cemetery
    near my apartment in Reykjavik since it was the closest thing
    to a park in my area. The moss was lovely to walk and bounce
    on while listening to the security guard who was also a cellist.

23. Lemon was a famous character in Sarajevo. Surrounded
    by myth and mystery, no one could ever forget the first
    time they saw him. The image of Lemon walking toward
    the old town pushing a shopping cart with Taxi written on
    it during the war is a true story witnessed by friends and
    colleagues.

24. I was asked to help out at a private school in Sarajevo for a
    few weeks. It was there I heard my first — pop and yelp —

a dog stepping on a landmine. Rats were later trained to help demine because people cared less if they died.

26. The first half of this poem takes place in St. Judes Anglican Church in Oakville, Ontario, Canada and the second half takes place atop the Holiday Inn in Sarajevo, Bosnia and Herzegovina, where my friend Darko and I were watching a funeral.

27. There was a small bar in the centre of Sarajevo for local artists. It was in a tiny house in a courtyard that most people had no idea existed. It was full of busts of Tito and all the tablecloths and curtains featured the cartoon characters Tom and Jerry. The owner found them for cheap and never changed them in the years I visited it with local poets like the late Admiral Mahić.

43. When I was living in Duhok, Kurdish North of Iraq, I would go for very long walks after school when it began to cool off. On the main road's sidewalk there was a massive wooden fish about ten feet long. In the two years I was there it was not moved, and no one could tell me why it was there.

47. My third poem about this horrible man — may age savage him.

50. *Evangelizare pauperibus misit* me means He has sent me to declare the good news to the poor

51. A selection of Émile Petitot's words from his monographs. This was originally part of a much longer chapbook about him, but I think this single page and the title says it all.

56. Oriel in this piece is a window — not a misspelling of oriole.

59. The children's art gallery in Baku, Azerbaijan, was so full of propaganda that I decided to mock it like a childish art critic.

61. I was invited to read in the Republic of Georgia and would practice my reading in the cemetery behind my hotel. Drunks would also hide there and chase me out when bored. It was a respectful enough dynamic.

73. During my more troubling times at my job in Arusha, Tanzania, I would always fall back on reading the American herpetologist Karl Patterson Schmidt's journal entries after being bitten by a snake called a boomslang. He thought it would not kill him. It did. The form of my piece is taken directly from the structure of his journal.

80. Blocks B and D are areas allocated to Tanzanian Tanzanite miners. They are death traps. The owner of the mine I went to with my father said it was safe, but every miner I met had broken fingers and was covered in scars. I made the mistake of going down into one, which meant holding onto a rubber hose similar to a garden hose in Canada. There were no other safety precautions taken. It was terrifying and a bloody foolish thing to do.

86. Ginny was the name of the helicopter that landed on Mars February 18th, 2021.

84–89. The Yellow Room is a small room in the Kigali Genocide Memorial. You cannot walk into this room and exit the same person.

In the final poem Amiikkiqtainagaa:

Arctic Tern — an old boat on the beach — left for children to play in.

Paulatuk can be broken into Paula, meaning *soot* and tuk or tuuq, meaning *a place where one finds something.*

Rodger — an old boat, wrecked and stuck on a sandbar about a half hour out on Darley Bay. It was a constant destination or resting point for me when I hiked out towards the Arctic when the bay was frozen.

Go to https://farhangbook1.com/ for videos, photos, reviews, endnotes and more.

Please purchase or stream
Bill Pritchard Sings Poems by Patrick Woodcock.
All 11 tracks are taken from poems in *Farhang Book I*,
two of which are read to Bill's music by the author.